THE MIKE KENDRICK BIOGRAPHY

THURSDAY'S
CHILD

THE MIKE KENDRICK BIOGRAPHY

THURSDAY'S
CHILD

Mike Kendrick & Simon W. Golding

Foreword by **Sir Richard Branson**

First published 2014 by DB Publishing, an imprint of JMD Media Ltd, Nottingham, United Kingdom.

ISBN 9781780913834

Printed and bound by Copytech (UK) Limited, Peterborough.

For my wife Anne and my sons; Myles, James and Robert.

Also to my lifelong friends who made so much of this possible.

For success you need patience, support and encouragement from those you hold dear.
For failure you need even more of the same.

And in memory of three friends who passed away during the writing of this book; Don Smith, Joy Cartwright and Roger Fox.

Contents

Foreword

Everything you read in this book is absolutely true, apart from the references to me, probably.

Mike has always been able to tell funny stories and can keep an audience roaring with laughter. He has a naughty sense of humour and does not shirk at delivering a rude and inappropriate punchline even in the most salubrious of circles.

Given Mike's lifestyle he can call on his life experiences that include derring-do exploits in the most remote places, expeditions across darkest Africa, death defying hot air balloon rides, world record attempts and airship trips in far-flung places. Add to this the fact that he is a world class, grade A flirt and you have a recipe for a collection of very funny and rather cheeky stories.

I have never fully understood why Mike gets on so well with the ladies. He has been married to Anne for over forty years. I have never understood that either.

This is a collection of very amusing anecdotes, punctuated by details of some seriously stressful situations and some sad stories too, covering the early days of ballooning up until the time we met and decided to go into business together. He certainly was a pioneer of early hot air balloon flights and the book tells of the terrible scrapes he got into, and out of . . . by the skin of his teeth.

He has the ability to embarrass a lot of people but I trust him to behave properly and regard him as a person of integrity.

Apart from that, I have more on him than he has on me!

Sir Richard Branson

Introduction

This is the story of a pioneer who literally breathed new life into one of the earliest forms of flight; hot air ballooning. This precarious pursuit was invented in France during the 18th century and reborn in the 1960s with the advent of bottled gas. It tells the tale of Mike Kendrick, who saw the opportunity for adventure and business when he purchased his first balloon, Thursday's Child.

It was a journey that lasted more than 30 years and stretched from the Black Country in the West Midlands to some of the most remote and untrodden areas of the world. In the late sixties, modern hot air ballooning began. Although modern is an inappropriate word to describe this very basic form of flight that seemed to attract early pilots prepared to risk everything in a desperate effort to get their feet off the ground. It was a 'make it up as you go along, fly by the seat of your pants' approach.

The first balloons were very simply constructed, compared to today's aerostats. It was an uncomplicated premise based on the indisputable laws of physics. Hot air rises and if you capture that in a big bag, then that bag, with a basket suspended beneath it, floats up into the air. It has no form of steering, is blown in an indeterminable direction by the wind, sucked up to great altitudes by clouds and the only method of landing is to use the basket and the bodies inside it as a brake as it smashes into the ground with a bone crunching certainty and uncertain outcome. Like most forms of developing flights, technology moved quickly and killed or injured people on its way, including Mike Kendrick's friends and associates. Everything about the early days of ballooning screamed 'DON'T DO IT!' But he did it anyway.

Ballooning was an elitist, upper class activity undertaken by the well-off, Pimm's drinking adventurists, until enter Mike Kendrick - the Black Country's working man's, real ale drinking adventure seeker!

Mike was one of those early balloon pilots and in Thursday's Child he tells the story of his life and the events that threatened it. From what he describes as a poor background, he forged ahead as a one-armed bandit mechanic, philanderer and gentleman of ill repute in the swinging sixties, when the term 'sex, drugs and rock 'n roll' was first adopted . . . and it has to be said the reality of that was embraced by him with enthusiasm.

The wealth that placed a silver spoon in his mouth at 12-years-old and helped catapult him into the centre of the sixties elite was then wrenched out in his later teenage years. Heart breaking personal tragedy forced him to find a new career and adopt a different attitude that would drive him forwards.

This book contains a love story describing his first encounters with his wife, Anne, with whom he has remained married for more than 40 years, and the support of his wife and children has allowed him to pursue his dangerous and often anti-social lifestyle. It details stories of his exploits, his successes and what he refers to as his glorious failures. He has experienced a lot of both.

Hilarious and incident-packed forays into Africa and beyond have left him with an affinity for the dark continent, a place he says that 'calls you back' as it has to this day, having secured a commitment from him to assist the under-privileged people of this planet.

He became a well-known media personality, as a balloonist – or balloonatic – in the seventies and eighties, making several TV adventure documentaries, appearing on many TV programmes and he became a nationally known figure when he tried, tried again and ultimately failed to reach the edge of space in a hot air balloon, which almost cost him and his co-pilot, Per Lindstrand, their lives.

Using his skills and experience as a PR and marketing executive, he was instrumental in making hot air balloons accepted as a serious marketing tool for publicity conscious clients, manufacturing balloons in the shape of Robinsons Barley water bottles and even a flying pint of beer which saw him taking Ozzy Osbourne aloft.

Many celebrities and even royalty have enjoyed his company and it was inevitable that when Sir Richard Branson and Mike Kendrick joined forces to form a partnership, it was to become the largest aerial advertising company in the world.

Chapter One

Balloons, Motorbikes and Cow Muck

My introduction into ballooning began in 1970 when I was MD of a public relations company in Birmingham. One of my clients was a company called Bellstaff. They manufactured clothes for the hunting, shooting, fishing and outdoor pursuits fans, which included the motorcycle or 'biker' market.

Myself and my colleague, and long time friend, Steve Laugharne, who was in charge of the Bellstaff account, had some hilarious times running focus groups for the bikers. It was an effort to determine what they regarded as the major factors which affected their purchasing decision in the procurement of motorcycle apparel. It was a large and important market.

We held most of the focus groups in a pub called the Mount Pleasant in Wombourne, West Midlands, and the bikers turned up in droves with the promise of free drinks and sandwiches.

This pub was well-known to myself and my drinking partners. We spent most Monday evenings there because the beer was good and Len, the landlord, provided a very good line in 'flour baps', a soft bread bun filled with cheese, onions and locally produced black pudding. Importantly, Len also produced his own spiced pickled onions that were simply unique and delicious. They could take your breath away but perfectly complemented the contents of the flour baps. We always consumed them with relish and enthusiasm.

Len agreed to host the bikers' event and we assumed that the drinks would be non-alcoholic as the riders, many with pillion passengers, had to drive home. Although this was before the drink driving breath tests, bikers did have a reputation for being responsible people with respect for the law and other road users. It has to be said that some of those attending did not look at all responsible, resembling scruffy, long-haired Hell's Angel types with rather menacing attitudes and a slightly frightening appearance. When talking to me, they stood very close with fixed, unblinking eyes that somehow seemed to demand that you should listen to them, take note and concentrate on what they were saying. It was a little intimidating, but I learned later that this was a common habit as most of the time they wore helmets and this was the way to help them communicate with each other.

'I'll have quadruple rum and black,' said Mick. 'And a Babycham and Cherry B, in the same glass, for the misses.'

'In the same glass?' the landlord enquired.

'Yes,' said Mick, adding, 'her likes both and I can't be bothered to come back every time. Anyway, after three or four she won't care what she drinks. You could give her a glass of petrol and she wouldn't know the difference.'

I wondered if this focus group was going to work. I instructed the landlord to only serve singles in future.

Deciding that they were a nice, if different type of person, we switched the camera on and began to learn about them and their lifestyle. The bikers were not told that we represented Bellstaff, in order to get honest and unbiased input. The point was to record what the bikers thought of the main brands in the market in terms of price, value for money, fashion, quality and any other factors that affected the buying decision. It would give an overall view of where Bellstaff stood, alongside the competitors. Of critical importance to the research was to ask the group which brands answered the major buying requirements. All known motorcycle clothing manufactures were represented by a box. If the bikers thought any of those manufacturers answered a specific problem, we would place that in the relevant box. This would give us an idea which of the brands the bikers felt offered value for money, quality, durability and so on. Finally there was a box that stated, 'No brand answers this specific problem.' If anything went into this box it was a potential bonus since it identified a problem the bikers associated with the purchase of motorcycle apparel that no brand offered an answer to. This would give the opportunity for Bellstaff to create a new product that could lead the industry, since it appeared that no brands was currently offering a product that solved a specific problem that had been identified by the potential buyer.

However, it was quite a rare thing to discover, but on this occasion we did just that.

In the box that stated; 'No brand does this' it seemed that the major concern was that motorcycle trousers all leaked at the crutch.

An open debate followed in order to validate this specific point. No one in the room would disagree with that fact. One middle-aged well spoken gentleman, a Harley Davidson rider, stood up and stated that when a rider sits on a saddle it obviously creates a depression on the seat. He continued to explain that during times of precipitation a resulting puddle can form around the rider's seat that could lead to dampness in the crutch area if the garment is not fully waterproofed.

Mick, who had neatly circumvented my 'single drinks only' instruction and was now sitting at a table with four single rum and blacks in front of him, shouted, ' he means your bollocks get wet' and added, 'and the wife's crotch!'

'That's not always a bad thing,' someone retorted to great laughter.

'It is when I'm sitting with my back to her,' someone else joined in, 'doing a ton with both hands on the bars . . .'

It went on and on and was degenerating into a rather drunken, bawdy session with Steve and I exchanging nervous glances as we shut off the cameras and closed the bar. We had got what we needed and what we both thought was some invaluable feedback.

As the pub emptied we sat quietly with a pint of Banks's bitter and flour baps and reflected on what we had collected. We had some great stuff that should impress the client and provide useful material for a new publicity campaign.

I took a sip of my bitter and quietly contemplated on a successful and exciting day. It appears to be a habit of my life that at these moments of quiet, contented reflection, it tends to signal a change in mood and leads to panic and often devastation.

As Steve bit into the flour bap and took a deep swallow of the local ale, he popped one of Len's pickled onions into his mouth. The combination of malt vinegar and spices took his breath away and his sharp gasp rammed the onion into the back of his throat to block his airway. I watched, I admit, with some initial amusement at his discomfort as Steve began to rock backwards and forwards, unable to breathe and then began panicking, his arms flailing and his face slowly turning blue. The bar staff and remaining customers sat there frozen in horrified silence as his now wildly gesticulating body began to thrash around the room. I grabbed him and sat him back in his chair as he went a deeper shade of blue, resembling a Smurf, and he was beginning to lose consciousness. I started slapping him on his back, gently at first and then viciously and very hard. He was now making a very loud rasping noise, in an effort to take a breath but nothing worked. He was heading towards unconsciousness and was in trouble, there was no doubt about it. In a panic myself, I pressed his stomach using the Heimlich manoeuvre that I had read about somewhere and finally hit him again on the back with such force I thought I may have injured him. In a quite spectacular manner, the onion came out down his nose, still in one piece and dropped on his plate alongside the half-eaten flour bap.

Everyone stared in total silence, including myself. Steve actually recovered in seconds and finished his pint and bap off with ease. The onion, after its momentous journey, just sat alone on his plate. Steve nonchalantly pushed it away saying 'I think I'll leave that.'

* * *

So I was driving north, from my office in central Birmingham, to the head office of Bellstaff which was based in Stoke-on-Trent, to present my findings to the MD. That journey took me along the M5, when the traffic was halted and a queue formed. The cause of this queue was a hot air balloon. At that time, in the seventies, it was a rare sight. It was a beautiful orange and blue balloon floating alongside the motorway at about 100 feet in the air. There were only a handful of balloons in the UK at that time and every driver had slowed down, captivated by the spectacle. I later learned that the hot air balloon belonged to Roy Midwinter (of Midwinter Potteries fame) and was called Thursday's Child. I learned that because, not long after, I bought it from him.

I presented my research to the Bellstaff MD, explaining that the major perceived problem with the biker's market was that motorcycle trousers leak at the crutch. I reasoned that if the company could develop a product that would combat this then Bellstaff would have a product that no other manufacturer was offering and would be readily accepted into the marketplace.

The MD told me I was talking rubbish, that the bikers were obviously drunk and didn't know what they were saying. He explained that the company manufactured a line of trousers with welded seams that did not leak and that my research was total 'crap'. I argued that they may well have a garment that solved this problem but the fact was the bikers did not know about the product. It needed to be clearly communicated to them. I presented him with a black and white advert which simply stated 'Bellstaff - Our trousers do not leak at the crutch!' The advert was a basic statement that was a precursor of the modern day's 'it does what is says on the tin' legend. It worked and revolutionised the sales of Bellstaff trousers at a time when the company was struggling.

Towards the end of the meeting the Bellstaff MD mentioned that they were due to exhibit at the Isle of Man TT races that year and the company needed to get its name out there. He asked me to come up with some branding ideas for the event. New ideas are the stock in trade of the PR man and have to come thick and fast. I suggested we put the company name on one of these new hot air balloon things – they stop traffic – everybody halts to look at them. He asked me if it was possible and I told him I would find out. And I did!

A researcher within my office found the name of two balloonists that owned a balloon named Aquarius. In early 1974 I drove down to Buckinghamshire, near Stowe, to meet Giles Hall and John Gore. I had already spoken to them about attending the Isle of Man TT event, with Aquarius. They explained they would be able to attach a large Bellstaff banner on the balloon for the event and they were keen to get the job. The plan was to inflate the balloon and keep it on a tether line at strategic points on the island to maximise exposure to the public and television cameras. We met at a rather nice house, with a swimming pool, where they were living and took a few minutes to agree the fee of £400, including producing the banner, attending the event for three days and flying the balloon twice daily. Knowing next to nothing about hot air balloons I agreed to take a flight. I did not tell them that I had a very real fear of heights.

The balloon was made ready in the grounds of Stowe School, based at Stowe House, formerly the country seat of the Dukes of Buckingham and Chandos.

I watched the process with great interest. They started by dragging the basket off a small trailer and attaching the burner. They then unwrapped the balloon envelope and spread it out. I became aware that I was inappropriately dressed in an office suit and shiny shoes, noting that the pilot John Gore and the inflation crew were attired in wellington boots and had heavily gloved hands. The crew grabbed the mouth of the balloon and started flapping the balloon material until the envelope was half-full with cold air. John Gore then entered the envelope through the mouth and went to inspect the inside asking me to join him. He got to the crown of the balloon and explained that the top of the envelope was held in place by Velcro and secured by twine. On landing the air needed to be let out of the balloons as fast as possible so a 'rip line' was connected to the Velcro panel. This ran to the basket so the pilot could pull the rip line at the point of landing. It all sounded a bit dangerous and Heath Robinson to me, but I felt I could not duck out at this point.

The crews were appointed to their positions, ready for the inflation. There was a crown line person. His job was to hold on to a line that ran from the top of the balloon and keep it down for as long as possible, until he was instructed to 'bring it in' to the basket. Other crew members were assigned as basket crew two and were to be 'cremation Charlies', aptly named as will be described.

The pilot then lit the burner, told the cremation Charlies to take their positions at the entrance of the balloon mouth, facing the burner. They did so, donning hats and gloves. To my astonishment John Gore then pointed the burner at them and opened up the valve. A 12 foot flame shot towards them and I knew immediately where the name cremation Charlie had come from. I could not believe why they were not instantly incinerated. After several long blasts from the burner they were called out of the mouth of the balloon as the inflation proceeded, the burners filling up the envelope with warm air. The cremation Charlie crew emerged from the mouth of the balloon, minus their eyebrows, to take station at the basket.

Finally the pilot shouted 'in with the crown' and the crown man walked towards the basket with the crown line in hand as the huge yellow and red balloon rose majestically to a standing position and the pilot instructed 'hands on' to the six basket crew.

John then invited me into the basket, I clambered aboard and was given a very clear but short briefing. 'Hold on to these rope handles,' he said sternly, adding, 'Don't touch the propane cylinders and don't get out of the basket until I tell you to, even after we have landed.' The latter instruction was a little obvious, I thought. I was hardly likely to get out of the basket before we landed!

The basket crew were told 'hands off', lifting their hands, and weight, from the basket to check if the balloon was ready to lift-off and more heat from the burners was applied until the pilot thought the balloon was light enough to rise into the air, this process was repeated four or five times.

Finally he said 'hands away' and we ascended quietly and smoothly. I looked out at the splendid Stowe School below and the beautiful Buckinghamshire countryside, revealing itself beneath the basket, the wonderful rural view of rolling hills to wide open vales, from lush wooded valleys to meandering rivers. We climbed higher into a clear English evening blue summer sky. It was absolutely breathtaking. Another roar of the burners brought me back to reality.

John produced an OS (Ordinance Survey) map and, pointing at a spot on the map said, 'This is where we are. You're navigating.'

Actually I was not fazed by OS maps. I had got used to reading them while doing local rallies and treasure hunts at the Black Horse car club, in Shropshire during the late sixties in my Ford Prefect 105. Then later in a, really cool at the time, Triumph Herald convertible – black interior, wooden steering wheel, twin Pifco exhaust. It was the dogs!

I could follow the flight path OK but realised that if I looked straight down my vertigo kicked in. I was alright if I looked across. This would apply right through my ballooning career. My kids could never understand why I could not handle heights. I had previously embarrassed them at the top of the Eiffel Tower, where I plastered myself against a wall, unable to move and more recently, at my wife's insistence, when I walked the Sydney Harbour Bridge which resulted in me having to hold the hand of the male guide for the entire way. It was horrendous and humiliating.

My initiation flight was about to come to an end. After a little over an hour John announced we were descending and that he was looking for a landing area. John was concentrating hard and asked me to look out for horses and power lines, a standard request for all passengers, you can never have too many eyes on the landing site.

Now, at around 100 feet, he pointed at a field telling me he was going to try for that one. 'Try!' I thought. 'What do you mean try!' I didn't realise that, in the early days of ballooning, landing was an imprecise science.

'We have about 10 knots of wind on the surface,' John shouted (not including the knots in my stomach), 'so there might be a drag. I will have to go in hard as the field is short. Just before we hit, get down in the bottom of the basket.'

Hit! 'Christ,' I thought, 'I believed we were landing – not hitting!' The ground came up at an alarming rate and we smacked into it with me crouching in the bottom of the basket, experiencing what I thought were the last moments of my life. As the balloon basket went on its side the envelope acted, in the 10 knot wind, like an enormous sail, dragging the basket behind it as John pulled the rip line, which opened the Velcro panel at the top of the balloon to let the air out. Unfortunately the ground was wet and cows had been grazing on it until very recently. So we sailed across the field, the basket was dragging behind the envelope, collecting a slurry of liquid cow shit that flew into the basket, up the arm of my business suit as I was lying prone and dumping it on my nice shirt, in my hair and over my face.

The balloon finally stopped and I was told I could get out of the basket, which I did and stood there in my best suit and shoes, covered in cow dung and feeling a complete prat. Whilst I felt happy and relieved to have survived a trip in this most precarious mode of transport, I was also enthralled at the whole experience, the danger and the entire silliness of the thing, hanging in a basket below a bag of hot air. It was ridiculous, fascinatingly so. I was now a balloonatic. I had to get one! I also had an inkling that these aerostats had a future in marketing terms and my mind was working overtime on the branding possibilities.

I set about finding as much as I could about ballooning. I discovered that balloons were registered aircraft and you needed a pilot's licence to fly them. This involved a serious amount of work and dedication. You needed to pass theoretical exams on air law, aerostatics, navigation and meteorology.

The latter was probably the most daunting. Balloons were almost entirely dependent on the weather and in those days you needed an almost degree depth of knowledge on the subject in order to understand and appreciate the elements that could affect a hot air balloon's flight. Not just the question of cloud types but weather fronts, thermal activity, wind speeds, technical elements like saturated and dry adiabatic lapse rates, anabatic and adiabatic winds and a plethora of other conditions that were completely unknown and alien to me. Hot air balloon pilots also needed to understand the local effect the weather had on the ground surface and the turbulence created by hills and mountains, valleys, rivers and buildings. All lessons I was to learn the hard way.

Air law was just a question of swatting. It's a little like the Highway Code but more complicated. Like yachts on the water, balloons had right of way over powered aircraft but this did not mean we could fly at will, expecting everyone else to get out of the way. We had to observe the rules of the air and there are thousands of them.

The aerostatics exam really meant understanding how lighter than air balloons work, so you appreciate the limitations and do not injure yourself, your passengers, other people in the air and the public on the ground. Another element was the landowners in whose fields you set the balloon down, always without prior permission. It also included fuel management, flight briefings, maintenance of the aircraft and general safety rules.

Navigation was easier. There were no on board transponders or navigation aids for balloons in those days. You simply forecast the wind strength and direction at various altitudes, drew a 'V' shaped sector on an OS map, from the point of take off, and informed the chase crew where you thought you would be after an hour's flight.

In winds above 7 knots, most of the time the chase crew got lost and were unable to keep up with the balloon so there was a standard procedure to follow. After landing the pilot would establish the balloon's position and using the OS map co-ordinates, call in the latitude and longitude coordinates to a pre-agreed telephone number. Normally, in my case, this was my mother's house. The balloon crew and the chase crew would both call in. This often meant long delays, since landing in the middle of nowhere meant the pilot had to walk to the nearest telephone box or ask a friendly farmer to use their phone. Since most flights were taken shortly after dawn, when wind speeds were more favourable, it was not always a simple task to find anyone awake at that time. It was the early days of ballooning and there was no ground to air radio to direct the chase crew and mobile phones had not yet been invented.

I was a busy public relations executive and if I was to become a balloon pilot the commitment to this process was not going to be easy. Apart from the time needed to pass the written examination, I also needed to learn how to fly. I would need to fly 35 hours as a PUT (Pilot Under Training), which would include two instructor flights with pilots appointed by the CAA (Civil Aviation Authority) as instructors and a check out flight by a CAA appointed examiner. Finally, and most daunting, a solo flight, meaning without an instructor or passenger, that was monitored from the ground by a CAA appointed observer. The problem was that there were only a handful of balloons in the UK and I needed to find one, with a pilot, to teach me how to fly.

John Gore came to the rescue. I think he recognised that I thought the commercial applications of hot air balloons were endless and that I could possibly find him work, to pay for his hobby, as I did with the Bellstaff Isle of Man contract.

So on the October 13 1974 John Gore brought Aquarius to Bridgnorth, Shropshire, to begin my training in earnest. My first training flight was from the Bridgnorth Golf Club practice ground, which nestles in the Severn Valley, beside the river. I had assembled a team of friends to help with the inflation and John briefed them carefully as we had never done this before. In fact, many of these friends were to join this journey of discovery over the next two decades.

As we ascended at nine o'clock in the morning, we left Bridgnorth Low Town to climb the cliff face, passing the cottages dotted on the steep cliff side climbing to High Town and onwards to hover above the historic town centre. The beauty of this picturesque little town unfolded below me in a way that can only be found by quietly hanging, almost still, above it in a basket, allowing silent reflection that only this mode of transportation can afford.

In the centre of the town, I examined the two churches that dominate its architecture, at each end of the High Street, which was built to a width which facilitated turning around a coach and six horses. In the middle of the High Street was the arched town hall which had stood for 400 years and I reflected on the fact that I had attended that town hall when I was 16 and was fined two shillings for a motorcycle offence. To the west were the ruins of the medieval castle and a little further along was Pan Pudding Hill where Oliver Cromwell built ramparts in order to fire cannons at the castle during the English Civil War. To the east, the River Severn was meandering her way to Ironbridge and beyond, shrouded in mist on this perfect autumnal English morn.

The sudden and huge roar of the one million BTU (British Thermal Unit) burners snapped me back to reality and I was reminded that we were suspended a 1,000 feet above the ground in a basket and were going to need to land on or hit the ground soon. I was allowed to use the burner in my first attempts to 'fly straight and level', but John handled the landing which was hard but uneventful.

I asked John what, in ballooning terms, was a good landing and he told me, quite matter-of-factly, 'any landing that you walk away from is a good landing.'

It was a beautiful flight but I was to learn that during these early days of lighter than air expeditions, ballooning could best be described as periods of utter joy, punctuated by moments of pure terror.

Getting training flights was very difficult and I only managed four flights during 1974. Balloons and pilots were few and far between. You had to be prepared to go anywhere at any time to find flights. At weekends my wife Anne and our two sons, Myles and James, aged five and four respectively, would need to leave the house at 3am to travel with me to a field 40 or 50 miles away, arriving before dawn to make a flight. Favourable flying conditions and light winds are more likely at dawn and dusk but we would often arrive to find the flight had been cancelled due to weather problems and then we simply came home. Those early morning cancellations and wasted journeys were frustrating and there was an element of futility that made me examine the devotion necessary to achieve this goal and explain it to myself and my family.

I made a commitment to do it and my family made a similar commitment to support my endeavour. It was a decision that would shape the future of our lives together. The dedication of my beloved Anne and the kids was the single biggest achievement of my life, bar none, and I salute and honour them for it. They shared the rewards and the fun, but also the heartbreaks, the dangers, my selfishness and the emotional turmoil and worry that I thrust upon them with some of my more outrageous exploits.

There were balloon groups springing up, in which would-be balloonists, led by a pilot, would form a club, each buying a share in a balloon and taking it in turns to fly. This looked a little time consuming and long winded to me. 'No,' I thought. 'There is only one way. I have to buy my own. My second thought, being a PR man was - who could I get to pay for it?'

Chapter Two

Thursday's Child

I let everyone I knew in ballooning circles, which was about four, that I wanted to buy a balloon. There was a UK manufacturer called Don Cameron who had established Cameron Balloons in Bristol. This Scottish balloonist had launched his company in 1971 and it is still going strong today. Although I could not afford to have a new balloon built by Cameron, I did not want to start a club, owning a share with several others was a viable option.

John Gore told me that there was a consortium in the Potteries that was selling their balloon so I journeyed an hour north to meet the leader of that group, a Mr Roy Midwinter of the internationally known Midwinter Pottery company. Roy explained that the consortium had a Western 65 balloon, with a banana rip, complete with trailer and four fuel cylinders. They had named the balloon Thursday's Child.

The number 65 after a balloon denotes the cubic capacity in thousands of cubic feet. So a Western 65 has 65 thousand cubic feet of hot air, which dictates the weight it can lift, in other words how many passengers. The 'banana rip' describes the Velcro secured deflation panel. In this case it was a pyramid shaped section of the balloon, above the equator, as opposed to a circular rip which took a section out of the topmost part of the envelope on landing. The Western balloon had been made by Wing Commander Jerry Turnbull, a pioneer of hot air ballooning. This balloon turned out to be the one that I had observed hovering above the motorway on my way to see my client Bellstaff.

Roy Midwinter told me that the name had come from the balloon group's first meeting, which took place on a Thursday. 'Thursday's child has far to go . . .' Appropriate, I thought, recalling the poem and it's a good job the meeting was not on the previous day – 'Wednesday's child is full of woe . . .'.

It occurred to me that ballooning was possibly a young single man's hobby, with all of its unpredictability, obvious risks of injury, the wing and a prayer philosophy, together with the anti social times of flights. I also thought that it was also not, at that stage, a 'working class' activity. Roy Midwinter was a middle-aged wealthy chief executive officer, John Gore a doctor of molecular biology, Giles Hall was very posh, his mother was Lady Something or other and Don Cameron was plainly an academic and scientist.

Enter me, a bloke from a Wolverhampton council house who left school at 15 without a single GCE.

The Roy Midwinter balloon group wanted £1,000 for Thursday's Child and I agreed to purchase all of the equipment, lock, stock and burner. Now all I had to do was to worry how I was going to pay for it, but I had an idea.

As a PR executive and, by that time, managing director of a PR agency, I had a list of very good and internationally known clients, but the one I had in mind was a local concern, Dudley Zoo. The zoo was a PR man's dream, offering wonderful opportunities for animal stories that appealed to the television and national press.

I had worked with the zoo for some time and loved interacting with the animals, it was fun getting TV slots and newspaper articles based on animal behaviour. However, it was also a serious business. Most zoos were in trouble, as they were simply not getting enough people through the turnstiles. Dudley Zoo needed 450,000 paying customers a year to make ends meet and was not achieving anything like that, so the very existence of the zoo and the animals that lived within its environs were under threat. The economics were horrible. It would be cheaper to slaughter the animals at the end of each summer and restock at the start of the season and it was not just about getting bums on seats. There was important work to do within a breeding regime that would protect various species against extinction during future years.

I knew how to get people in. It's called 'papering the house' and was something I had learned in the theatre – but that's another story. Papering the house is a term used to describe getting people into the theatre when a show is seriously undersold. There is nothing worse than a show playing to just a few members of the public. It was better to give tickets away and fill the place. The atmosphere would be better, the acts would enjoy it and word of mouth would kick in to sell more tickets.

So, for Dudley Zoo I papered the house. I devised a tour for various schools. We produced a slide show and members of the zoo's education department would give a lecture on the zoo activities and animal welfare. The show ended with a slide of Coco, an adorable chimp with a definite 'ahhhh' factor. I would then address the boys and girls explaining that Coco would love them all to visit them to meet him and all his animal friends, including Anak, his orangutan playmate, Victor the giraffe, Tanya the Indian elephant and all of the others. I explained that they were so keen to see all of the kids that the boss of the zoo had said they could all have free tickets. And Coco had come along to give the tickets to them. At that point Coco came into the school assembly hall clutching a bunch of tickets and started handing them out. He really was a little gem.

This marketing strategy was strong. No self respecting parent would allow a child to attend a zoo without them, so they needed to buy a ticket to accompany them. Hopefully, the child would create enough pester-power! 'Mommy, daddy, Coco has been to school and given me a free ticket to go and see him. Can I go? Can I? Can I?' This, I hoped, would be the usual greeting from most children on meeting their parents after school. The result? One free child with two paying parents.

It worked very well and the attendance figures multiplied almost immediately. I organised numerous media stories and developed a wonderful love for some of the animals, particularly Pepi, the giant chimpanzee, who grew to hate me with a vengeance. I had done so many photo calls with him to the point that he became bored when I approached his enclosure and would rant and rave at me, jumping up and down, stomping, beating his chest and screaming. The enclosure had a tiered concrete stepped viewing area that could hold several hundred people, protected from the apes by a moat. He would recognise me if I walked through the crowd, go into his aggressive threat mode and pick up anything in the enclosure to throw at me. When there was nothing left to throw he would crap in his hand and throw that at me. He was a reasonable shot too and several of the punters standing close to me would go home smelling a little ripe, with chimp poop stains about their person.

I asked the BBC to bring the legendary voice of the animals, Johnny Morris, to the zoo and promised them a good sequence. Johnny was the host of the 'must watch' television series Animal Magic. In those days they shot the film footage and Johnny would add voices to the animals, live in its Bristol studio as the show was broadcast. The first sequence we filmed was of Tanya the Indian elephant. Although Tanya had been in captivity at the zoo for thirty years she allowed Johnny on her back and he shouted instructions to her in an Indian dialect to which she responded instantly, moving logs and tree trunks and carrying them to new locations. What a memory! I was later to get her to hold my balloon down in the Dudley Castle courtyard for a photo call.

The BBC crew then moved to the ape house and its enclosure, and I said, 'Johnny, this is the gig. You move to the front of the moat with the camera behind you, eating an apple. Pepi will look at you and you can overlay a voice saying, "Can I have a bite of your apple, mate?" You then throw him the apple which he will start to eat. However, I will move to a position behind the camera and I guarantee he will throw it at you (well at me, to be honest). An extra voice-over from Pepi then saying, "Have it back, this apple is sour!" and we have a great bit of film.'

It sounded simple but an hour later we were on the umpteenth take.

Pepi was insisting on copulating with all of his females, multiple times, in full view of the audience and had thrown every moveable item from the enclosure at me. At least, I thought, after eating so much fruit and defecating so many times he can't produce any more crap so that was a blessing.

The BBC producer, George, emerged to declare we would give it one more take but I had underestimated Pepi's resolve. Having eaten at least a couple of pounds of green apples he made a massive effort to defecate one last time and empty the remains of his bowels into his hands. He then ran from the back of the enclosure and launched the festering mass into the air. Johnny and I knew what was coming and legged it, but George seemed unable to move and watched as the missile arched, high in the air over the moat, still in one piece, refusing to fragment, until it landed squarely on George's BBC shirt, BBC blue tie and BBC blue mohair suit, with a splattering smack.

George stood very still, expression unchanged, removed his black rimmed spectacles, to clean them and said, quietly and stoically, 'I'm completely covered in monkey shit.' 'The technical term is Igwano', remarked Johnny, with that telling and famous enigmatic smile across his face.

So it was with a history of getting the zoo a great deal of press and TV coverage that I propositioned John Shields, the manager of Dudley Zoo, with the idea of having a hot air balloon. I explained that Cameron Balloons had agreed to put Dudley Zoo on each side of the balloon in 10 feet tall letters with animal shapes running around the side. I thought we could use it for a lot of press calls, tethered flights in the castle keep and flights over the local area. I explained that hot air balloons were amazing media magnets and would create a lot of PR noise as everybody stopped to watch them. I had been doing quite a lot of work with a programme called Tiswas, a mad Saturday morning show hosted by Chris Tarrant. It had an enormous following, mainly five to15 year olds, as well as parents. In fact my two children, Myles and James, were featured on the first Tiswas promotional posters and I had a very good relationship with Chris dating back to the time he was a reporter with the local TV news.

I produced the budget, showing the price of stitching the zoo artwork on to the Thursday's Child envelope and the running costs of the balloon, insurance, fuel and maintenance. He went for it. Phew! I then completed the purchase and became the proud owner of the aerostat Thursday's Child. I immediately joined the British Balloon and Airship Club. We were in business.

We announced the arrival of the Dudley Zoo balloon to the press and planned a flight from the Dudley Castle keep. It was not possible to get airborne due to wind conditions, but we did manage to inflate the balloon and get Tanya, the old Indian elephant, to hold the balloon down with her trunk. So it was a nice story, although I could not entice Coco or Anak into the basket. They did not like the roar of the burner. Anak, a very lovable baby orangutan, was calmer than Coco but still would not come on to the basket. When we had deflated the balloon, Anak reached out to me, arms wide open. I picked her up and gave her a big hug and she gripped me fiercely, burying her head in my neck. It almost felt that she had been worried about me and was glad I was safe.

When I went home that night I entered the kitchen and my wife's eyes became very wide indeed. 'How did you get that?' she said, pointing to my neck accusingly. I looked in the mirror and was horrified to see what appeared to be a giant love bite. 'It was an orangutan,' I stuttered, adding 'honestly.' She realised not even I could have made that one up.

* * *

I was now the proud owner of Thursday's Child, which was an aircraft registered with the UK Civil Aviation Authority as G-AZBX. So on May 18 1975 I began training in my own balloon but, given the scarcity of balloons and the shortage of qualified pilots to fly with me, it took two years and a further 24 flights to get my licence. It was not without incident either. The purchase of Thursday's Child was to prove a defining moment in my life and I wondered if fate had decreed that it should be this way. I looked up my date of birth, May 9 1946, and discovered I was born on a Thursday. I was indeed a Thursday's Child and had far to go.

I was still living in Wolverhampton, although we had bought a pair of rather rundown cottages in Bridgnorth. We would have to wait for the tenants to move out and then a serious renovation project would follow before we moved in. While we were living in Wolverhampton the balloon and trailer were proudly parked in the driveway, inviting comment and, I have to say, a touch of wonderment amongst neighbours and people passing by. A chap called Tony Gough knocked on the door one evening and introduced himself as a balloon pilot and member of the Salamander group. Salamander, registration G-BANG, was a Cameron 84 (four people), built in a blue and orange check pattern which I had seen in the sky, from the Thursday's Child's basket, on a couple of occasions. Tony was keen to help me and we soon became friends as he nursed me through my training programme.

On my 29th birthday in 1975 we took Thursday's Child, now adorned with the Dudley Zoo branding, to Patshull Park, a stately home turned golf club just west of Wolverhampton to prepare for a morning flight. The inflation and chase crew was made up of mates who helped in return for the odd flight. It was Pete Mathews' turn today. He was an old friend and a builder who was renovating my cottages and was always up for some action. Years as a builder had given him a muscular and almost intimidating physique. We decided to inflate near the lake but I was a little unsure of the wind conditions and also concerned about the proximity of the lake, given that we were on sloping ground. I thought we may get some curl over. Curl over is best described as moving air (wind) that rushes faster up hill and creates turbulence once over the brow. It can be very dangerous for balloons, creating down drafts or up drafts which could cause envelope distortion, resulting in a sudden loss of lift. Obviously not something you would want on take off. Tony thought it would probably be ok. So we put the ground crew in position, Pete the hard man was appointed as cremation Charlie and we began to inflate. The inflation went perfectly, the crew came to the basket and I quickly went through the preflight checks.

'You have the retrieve number?' They nodded in agreement. 'You have money for the phone box?' Again they confirmed this. This was years before mobile phones and ground to air radios and the retrieve crew were reliant on keeping a balloon in view and following as best they could. It was essential that the retrieve crew and pilot carried some small change in the event that they lost sight of the balloon and had to use a phone box to call in.

It was slightly gusty so I needed to get away, one last visual check of the envelope, this was going to be great. It was my birthday and an adventure lay ahead.

'OK', I shouted. 'Flight time one hour, wind speed 10 knots, see you later. Hands off, hands on.' One final burn, the balloon became hot and light and was straining to get into the air. 'Hands away!' was my final instruction and we rose steadily but I knew immediately that we were in trouble.

The wind hit us at about 100 feet, but we kept rising until around 200 feet when the curl over kicked in, closing the mouth of the balloon and distorting the envelope, so I could not get any more heat into the balloon. We were going down and there was nothing I could do about it. I looked down and tried to estimate if we would hit the foreshore or go straight into the lake. In the end we did neither. On the edge of the lake was a group of dead trees, about 50 feet tall. The balloon envelope went heavily into them, the basket hitting the ground in front of them. The branches of the trees went straight through the envelope. As we hit the ground, with a ton of hot air still in the envelope, physics took over, the balloon became light for a second or two while hitting the ground and we sprang back into the sky. As the balloon rose the branches of the dead trees which had penetrated the envelope, slowly and rather gracefully took out the entire side of my precious balloon. Tony had switched the burner back on as we were rising. He was more experienced than I but I realised the inevitable conclusion of this flight as we rose up to 300 feet above the middle of the lake. The balloon was about to fall out of the sky and no preventative action could be taken to stop it.

For some inexplicable reason Pete took off his woolly hat, rolled up his shirt sleeves and shouted, 'I'm out of here!' as he prepared to jump overboard, into the lake, giggling nervously. I grabbed him as Tony shouted frantically, 'We'll make it to the shore!' We were totally out of control, with a badly ripped envelope, and the balloon descended rapidly to crash into a field adjoining the lake, with a bone-crunching smack that we were lucky to survive without serious injury. We felt very, very foolish. It did nothing to curb our enthusiasm for this form of flight. In fact, it spurred us on. It was a good derring-do story to tell our friends, as I moved on towards the ultimate objective – to become a pilot.

There was no doubt that ballooning was somewhat of an elitist activity and some felt it was a 'club' that was difficult to be accepted into, a distinct snob factor was firmly entrenched in this small and exclusive gathering of balloon enthusiasts. It did not go down at all well with my mates. They had noticed a growing band of sky gods emerging who seemed to talk a lot about the meteorological elements of balloon flying and the extreme flying conditions that they had somehow survived. 'Thought I was a goner and there I was at 10 thousand feet and the burner went out' would be a typical war story.

Some balloonists thought that plus-fours were the thing to wear and there was a propensity, amongst some of the ballooning fraternity, to adopt a slightly eccentric upper class persona. In some cases it was enough to wear a silly hat or some other accessory consistent with a person who undertook dangerous exploits that justified a level of stand-offishness and arrogance. I had news for them. The working classes were coming.

I was called one day by a chap who introduced himself as a pilot and made it plain that he was willing to give up a little of his valuable time to give me the odd flying lesson. I jumped at the chance, anything to help me to accelerate my quest to get to the point of a check out flight and become the captain of my own aircraft.

We had a flight scheduled that weekend but no pilot available, so I gave this new guy a call. I briefed the crew and we eagerly awaited the flight, my friend Rob Jones remarking 'I hope he's not a prat.' Rob was one of my oldest friends and he and the crew all got on famously with Giles Hall, John Gore and Tony Gough but my crew were all Black Country people and could not relate to individuals they regarded as 'up themselves'.

When the weekend came along I rang Birmingham Airport for the Met (weather) forecast and it did not look good, with high winds, rain and low cloud forecast. I called the aforementioned pilot and informed him that the flight would not be going ahead due to a high possibility of inclement weather. 'Oh, I wouldn't say that,' he pontificated in a rather self opinionated, don't argue with me tone. 'You never know until you get on site. Things can change suddenly. We can make a decision on the day.' As the flight was scheduled for that afternoon I went along with it and we all assembled on Enville Common, in foul weather conditions and waited for the so- called 'pilot' to arrive. Rob was looking grumpy and mumbling about going to the pub.

The pilot arrived, carrying a map and flight bag, and said, 'Good afternoon,' to the crew, then proceeded to unfold the air map and study it.

'We can't fly in this weather,' commented one of my crew.

'That is my decision,' said the pilot, cutting in curtly. He then stepped away from the basket, picked up some grass and threw it in the air to determine the wind speed, stared at the map again, looked in the direction the wind was coming from, then down wind and then at the cloud base, contemplated for a few seconds before stepping back to address us all. 'I have made a decision,' he said rather pompously. 'It is not flyable.'

'That's obvious,' said Rob Jones. 'The wind's blowing a gale, the cloud base is too low and it's pissing down!'

The man looked at him sternly, saying, 'I'm a pilot -'

'You're a prick,' Rob interjected and he left for the pub.

Consequently we never used this pilot again. He was probably going through a certain stage in his life having recently won his 'wings' as a qualified pilot and his enthusiasm may have outweighed his skill. He may be a perfectly nice guy nowadays, which is why I have not disclosed his name.

I spent the next year flying as often as possible and had some wonderful flights over the glorious Shropshire countryside, with its rolling hills and valleys, picturesque villages and friendly pubs that littered the county in abundance. I have to say, though, that the landings were always eventful. In anything more than a 5 knot wind the landing technique was not subtle at all. The only way to land was to deflate the balloon, using the rip line to pull open the Velcro panel at the top of the balloon, which opened up a large hole to let out the hot air when you were over the landing area. This frequently meant smacking into the field after briefing the passengers to get below the rim of the basket to prevent getting hit on the head by the burner, which was free floating above the basket. Although that was all changing as Don Cameron of Bristol Balloons and a new entry in hot air balloon manufacturing, Thunder Balloons Ltd in London, run by Dick Wirth and Tom Donnelly, were developing new ideas.

Hot air balloons were creating a lot of attention and we were often asked to attend shows and put on demonstrations of this fascinating, little understood form of flight. On one occasion we were invited to attend such an event in Stoke and Steve Laugharne and I set off to impress a potential new client. The site for the inflation was nothing more than a building site but we laid out Thursday's Child and flapped some air into the envelope. We were inexperienced and did not really know what we were doing. As it was a building site we had been issued with the requisite yellow plastic hard hats and I went into the mouth of the balloon while Steve manned the burners. Steve was briefed to open the gas valve, in short blasts on my signal. He had not operated a burner before and was familiarising himself with the valve tap whilst waiting for my hand signal. Unfortunately, while I was still in range of the burner, Steve inadvertently opened the valve and a 12 foot long, one million BTU, flame shot in my direction. My hair was fashionably long in the seventies and cascaded below the rim of the yellow hard hat. Those flowing locks disappeared in an instant along with my eyebrows and nose hair leaving a burned and frizzled mass of debris. I quickly staggered out of the balloon looking like a zombie, face blackened, my head smoking and smelling like a bonfire. The potential client and observers looked at me in complete horror, as I rubbed my head as all the burnt hair fell off. I removed the hard hat, showing off my Moe Howard haircut from The Three Stooges and looked at Steve. He was standing there, looking at the state of me and holding his crutch, tightly, in an unsuccessful attempt to prevent him pissing himself with laughter. I tried vainly, to pass the event off in a nonchalant, offhand manner in order to trivialise the incident and continue to present Steve and I as a team of entirely competent individuals. However the sight of me, still smoking, now bald from the ears down, did not portray the impression of complete professionalism. We never did get that contract.

New developments were exciting and inflation fans were now available which dispensed with the need for a cremation Charlie. The petrol engine-driven fan was placed at the mouth of the balloon to fill the envelope with cold air before the burners were switched on. Double burners were also being introduced which doubled the output power and double gimballed burners were coming in. This meant that the burners could be swung in all directions to make sure the heat went into the mouth of the balloon. Thursday's Child only had one single gimballed burner and, in windy conditions, it was sometimes impossible to get heat into the balloon. That often contributed to causing hard landings and even at altitude wind shear would bend the flame away from the mouth leading to some unscheduled and unwelcome fast descents that, with a single burner, could be difficult to arrest.

I remember one particular flight in Thursday's Child when I broke out of cloud at 1,500 feet, descending fast. I burnt all the way down, putting as much heat into the envelope as possible and still hit the ground with a terrible thud. Of course, I should never have been above the cloud in the first place. That was illegal. VFR (Visual Flight Rules) state that you should always be in sight of the ground but it was tempting to 'go on top' and sometimes in an ascent you never really knew how high you were going to get. Once the air inside the envelope was hot the balloon would just keep rising until the hot air cooled down, at which point it would stop ascending. It was always difficult to calculate at what height the balloon would stop and level out. Velcro rip balloons did a have a 'dump' near the equator of the envelope. The dump was a fabric window which, when opened by using a line connected to it, released or dumped hot air in order to arrest an ascent but they were never really efficient and definitely not fast-acting.

Importantly, a 'cow burner' was becoming available. This was an additional, slow opening burner to be used over livestock. It took away the sudden high decibel blast of the burner that could frighten them and was an important development. As balloonists, we were reliant on the goodwill of farmers. After all, we were always landing in their fields without prior permission. Most farmers, being the sporting types, welcomed us. Not all but most. The cow burner was later to be referred to as the 'whisper burner'.

A new support system for the burner was also developed. It was called a 'flexi-rigid' system. A flexi-rigid pole was strapped into each corner of the basket and held the burner frame permanently above the heads of the passengers. They were flexible enough to take the landing impact without breaking but rigid enough to hold the frame in place above the basket to avoid the burners crashing down on the heads of the people in the basket during landings.

Before the flexi-rigid system, the standard landing brief was to instruct the passengers to get down into the basket and hold on to the rope handles. This had caused some nasty injuries. A pilot called Stuart Ashby had problems when the Velcro rip had opened during flight. He briefed his passenger, his wife Helen, to prepare for a hard landing and to get down below the rim of the basket. When the balloon hit, very hard, she was in the bottom of the basket and her knees went into her face. She was very badly injured and needed a long stay in hospital and surgical treatment.

One fellow pilot I knew well, flying the Salamander balloon, realised he was in a fast descent and was going to hit a lake. He gave the standard briefing to his female passenger and they hit the water very hard. The pilot struggled to keep the balloon inflated as it careered at 15 knots across the lake with the envelope acting like a spinnaker. The balloon, with the basket submerged, went right across the lake and over a small island before going back into the water. As the basket went over the island, the water drained from the basket and the pilot realised he had been standing on his passenger during the process, almost drowning her. I spoke to that passenger some time later and she had vowed never to go near one of those 'bloody death trap' contraptions ever again.

So the development of a 'burner support' greatly improved the safety of our balloons.

There was also talk of a new rip system. A 'parachute rip'. Basically, it was a huge parachute shaped 30 foot piece of material that fitted on the inside, at the top of the envelope. The top or 'crown' of the balloon had a slightly smaller hole and the parachute would fit snugly up against it, effectively plugging the hole and held in place by the pressure of the hot air inside the envelope. If you pulled the parachute rip down on landing it would deflate the balloon. Importantly, it could be used in flight to dump air out and would simply snap back into place if you released the rip line.

Ballooning and, more importantly, landing was going to get a whole lot safer with the introduction of inflation fans, two or three, fixed in place, multi gimballed burners and a parachute rip.

Our unusual form of flight was also growing in popularity and needed this type of development to increase safety. Already two balloonists had been killed. Mike Adams and Mike Sparks were flying near Birmingham when the Velcro rip opened in flight, deflating their balloon and sending them crashing to their deaths. This fatality was a huge blow to the ballooning community. We were a small group of balloon enthusiasts in the UK and all knew each other well. It was a wake-up call. We were all getting a little blasé about flying and accepted broken bones, cuts, bruises and narrow escapes as an inevitable consequence of this type of activity. But this was different, two of our friends, young men, took off in their balloon for a great adventure and were now dead.

New, safer, easier to fly and, critically, easier to land balloons with powerful burners and much improved fabric were going to be the aerostat of the future.

I wanted one.

Chapter Three

Back to the Beginning

I formed my balloon company called Lighter Than Air Ltd with the intention of making it an aerial advertising specialist company, adding new clients as quickly as I could. I was planning to present to F W Woolworth. If I got a new contract I would have a stable of two balloons which would make Lighter Than Air Ltd a viable business. My company only had one office and a small room for Joan, my secretary, and I knew I would have to relocate soon. I also had a new business starting with my young brother Jonathan. He had joined the Goodyear tyre company in Wolverhampton after he left school. Luckily, I had a friend who worked at Goodyear and she found him a position in an exciting department, the racing division. Jonathan was dealing with racing drivers and managers. He, like our father and myself, had the keen nose of an entrepreneur and believed that there was a market selling second-hand racing car tyres 'as used by James Hunt' and the like to aspiring young racers. It was moderately successful but had no real long-term future. I was glad to have Jonathan around me, we had recently lost our father in the most tragic of ways when Jonathan was only 16 and we were soon to lose our mother, aged 54, to cancer. It was a troubling and traumatic time for all of us.

Thinking about it, my entire life had been somewhat traumatic and, as a child and teenager, it had been a roller-coaster of emotional incidents with great highs and very deep lows. My dad was a slightly built man with a big personality, a risk taker with a bent for the world of entertainment. He was always impeccably dressed. Clean shaven, save for a well trimmed moustache, and he abhorred what he referred to as 'filthy language'. My mother was quite the opposite, she enjoyed swearing and was wonderfully and enjoyably neurotic, often turning a day-to-day drama into a full-blown, action packed crisis and a whole family row. Home was always a noisy and intense environment.

I was born in a prefabricated bungalow, homes which were necessary after World War II to house a growing population. Prefabs could be erected quickly, in sections, and were designed for a lifespan of 15 years. There are still some left to this day, including the one I lived in at 55, Lincoln Green, Wolverhampton.

Dad would play the piano in pubs for 10 shillings a night to supplement the family income, after working a shift at an aircraft factory. He was not given the chance to 'join up' during the wartime years as the work he was doing was considered essential to the war effort. He was always miffed about that. We then moved to a council house on a new estate in a suburb of Wolverhampton. It was a pleasant area and the house was built on the edge of fields, which were the playgrounds for me, my elder sister Viki and the other kids on the estate. The playing fields were often a happy release to escape the pandemonium and domestic rows that frequently visited our household. I don't think that the long-term effects of domestic rows on children were fully understood in the 1950s and my sister recalls that we often hid in a metal cupboard whilst our parents argued and screamed at each other. The rows were never violent in physical terms, but were always frightening to us children. I think dad was insecure, probably resulting from his childhood experiences. His father left him and his six older sisters when he was aged 7 to run off with another woman and live under an assumed name. It was a hanging offence in those days and dad was never to hear from his father again for many years, until he found him living in Ireland 40 years later.

I think the feeling of abandonment and the hardships that inflicted upon him and the family affected him greatly. He suffered from attacks of deep depression and insecurity and was subject to black, suicidal moods. However, most of the time he was a jolly person with an ambition to succeed. We always had a good Christmas and my sister and I would always wake up on Christmas morning to an array of brightly wrapped gifts. He told me later that he wanted to make sure we did not experience the heartaches that he went through as a child, without a father figure, in the ravages of the post World War I period. He once sadly recalled that on one Christmas morning his only presents were a comb and an orange.

Dad's sisters, who also recalled this time, told me that he ate the orange (actually a treat in those times), put some paper over the comb and hummed through it making music. This was a forerunner of the modern day kazoo and he played all of the Christmas carols, having a wonderful time. There is a lesson there, somewhere.

We were poor but dad was a trier and would take us to the seaside occasionally when funds would allow. It was always Rhyl in north Wales where we would go on spec, finding bed and breakfast accommodation when we got there. We only went for two or three days, climbing into a very old Austin 7 at five o'clock in the morning to begin the mini holiday. An enduring memory of one such trip still haunts me to this day. My big sister, Viki, elder by 13 months, and I were looking forward to the seaside and we arrived on Rhyl promenade early in the morning. While driving along the prom the suspension leaf springs fell off the ancient car and it came to a grinding halt. I remember looking back along the promenade road to see that a woman had dismounted from her horse to pick up the pieces that were lying on the road and kindly handed them back to dad. It was obviously a serious breakdown and it cost most of the money dad was carrying to repair the car. My recurring vision is standing on the beach with my sister in her little bathing suit holding a tin bucket and spade in her hand. It was windy and the sand was stinging our legs as it blew across the beach. I can see her face and her grimace as she stood there, trying to look as though she was enjoying herself, knowing we had to go straight home as soon as the car was repaired. We had no money left to stay a night. To this day, the vivid memory and our disappointment still haunt and upset me.

I was in awe of the dedication of dad's six sisters in bringing up their young and only brother. One of them, my auntie Edna, a very intelligent and beautiful person, gave up a scholarship to work in a factory in order to bring money into this destitute family. The alternative was to put the children in the Cottage Homes, a sort of children's care facility of the day. Aunty Edna was having none of it.

By the time we were aged 7 and 8 my father had now started running dances at the Cock Inn, Bilston, attended by the rocking and rolling Teddy Boy fraternity of the 1950s. He had formed the Vic Kendrick's Hawaiian Rhythm Band, which I remember well, featuring at several working men's clubs in the area. The band provided a musical and comedy act for which there was a big demand at this time of great austerity. He went on to form the Midland Entertainment Agency which booked acts for local clubs and theatres. Entertainment was in our blood and I frequently accompanied dad to the Wolverhampton Hippodrome to witness the latest of the variety shows, which were coming to an end in theatre land. I can remember seeing Laurel and Hardy live on stage and I can still recall their act. In those days, variety theatres were desperate to keep the public interested and often supported the show by featuring still scenes of nude ladies. Twenty completely naked ladies would be revealed as the curtain opened, positioned in manikin style poses. They were not allowed to move a muscle, staying perfectly still while the auditorium ogled them.

It was around this time that dad contracted a serious physical illness that would require radical stomach surgery. He lived with it for some time until I witnessed an ambulance arriving to take him to hospital. He weighed under six stone and the ambulance men did not bother with a stretcher but simply picked him up, like a baby, and carried him down the stairs.

It looked very bad and I knew from the family conferences between my mother and the sisters that had brought him up without a father that they thought there was a good chance he would not make it. Kids hear much more than you think they do when a family is in crisis and discussions, not meant for young ears, are conducted in hushed and urgent whispers. It was not just a question of the impending surgery but whether or not dad had the strength of mind to get over this.

In other words, with his depressive condition, it was questionable if he would have the mental will to pull through. The surgeons removed two thirds of his stomach, put him in a bed and we waited. We waited for three days for him to wake up, with dark thoughts of death and funerals, unable to get any comfort from the medical profession. They could really tell us nothing. Then a strange thing happened. My mother contacted a faith healer and asked her to try to help in this desperate situation.

They went to the hospital together and the healer placed her hands on the operation wound and said, 'This man will wake in three days and get better.' And he did! Although my parents were not religious, faith healing was to play a part in their future as my father attempted to find answers to his crippling bouts of depression and mental turmoil.

Business was doing well and expanded into supplying pinball machines and one-armed bandits to working men's clubs and he even bought his own cafe, The Flamingo. Suddenly we were rich! We were still living in a council house and while our parents had no particular ambition to move, that matter was to be taken out of their hands in a most unpleasant manner.

We had already fallen out with our neighbours, the Cadmans, something to do with the noise generated by the piano, but were now being forced out by a sensationalised story appearing in a national Sunday newspaper, The Sunday Pictorial. I think to this day the Cadmans had something to do with this.

The reporter had presented himself to my dad wanting to cover a story about a council house tenant making good. He even arranged for a photograph of us kids waving from the shiny new Humber Super Snipe parked outside in the road. Unfortunately, what appeared was an exposé type of story depicting a man earning £60,000 per year (which was untrue and a great deal of money in the sixties) and implied that we were taking advantage of living in a house that was badly needed for a less fortunate family. It was devastating and the household was bombarded by hate mail, threats and begging letters with visits from people toting rent books showing arrears and impending eviction. Destitute mothers with children in hand would stand outside on the door step and thug-like looking men would appear, demanding money with menaces. My father's depression kicked in again and I can remember wrestling with him again, on the floor, to remove the pills and bottles of alcohol from him in his suicidal cry for help. There was no alternative, we had to move.

Just before this I had left school at 15 under a bit of a cloud. I was not expelled but rather asked to leave. There was no point in staying on at school anyway. Although I was in the Alpha (GCE) stream, I was a hopeless student and the school was not a good one, with a culture of fighting, bullying and public caning. There was a boy named Trevor Barnbrook who lived on our council estate. He was caned regularly for wearing tight fitting Teddy Boy trousers called drainpipes. Sadly, he didn't have any other trousers so could do nothing about it. I hated every second of it and was relieved when they asked me to go.

At this school, power was the key and the more badges you could hold the better – dinner monitor, prefect, anything that could put you in a position of control of something. One job I got was looking after the keys for the school library, a wooden construction in the assembly hall. As it was a mixed school it offered opportunities for a select few to liaise with the girls. I used to rent it out, not for money, but for other currencies like the odd chocolate bar, someone to do my homework or getting picked for the football team. There was no penetrative sex going on, of that I am sure, just meetings with girls you liked, to do what adolescent youths do.

The problem was it escalated from there a little with the introduction of a flat in which to educate the girls in the subject of domestic science.

The girls' head teacher, Mrs Murdoch, ran this facility and had the forethought to introduce another item of equipment to further the girls' domestic education. A bed! I was caught red handed by Mrs Murdoch with a pretty student and my days of scheming were numbered.

I joined my dad's company as a trainee mechanic maintaining the gambling fruit machines, or one-armed bandits as they were better known, and would travel around the Midlands with my uncle Wilf. He was a qualified welder but could turn his hand to anything and it was his job to fix the gaming machines when they broke down. The one-armed bandits were purely mechanical in the early days of gaming machines, but the pinball machines were highly complex electrical devices with miles of different coloured wires and circuit boards. My uncle Wilf was recruited into the business to maintain and repair all types of gaming machines.

Wilf Leach was a hugely intelligent man but colour blind and he was always asking me 'what colour is this?' and 'is this wire the same colour as this?' I used to play snooker with him at the working men's clubs and watch him potting the brown, thinking it was a red. I always ended up a few pounds better off.

We moved from the council house to a nice large bungalow named Morinda. It was palatial compared to the tiny council house. It had been superbly appointed and decorated at my mother's direction. It boasted one of the first colour televisions installed and the gardens had been expertly landscaped. My dad's business was growing and he moved the office from the back of the Flamingo cafe to a small block of offices.

I was now mobile, having a Triumph Tigress scooter. It was the swinging sixties, dubbed the permissive society and I took full advantage of that in the most ungentlemanly and irresponsible way possible. I was now managing dance venues with live bands such as Slade, who were to become very famous. It was cool or 'fab' as was the vernacular in the sixties. My dad was rich, had progressed, car wise, to owning Bentleys and, if I was not careful how I handled myself, I could become a spoilt, arrogant rich kid with the morals of an alley cat. I wasn't careful and I did to my eternal embarrassment and shame, degenerate into that unsavoury character. I turned into a morally bankrupt precocious, pompous git and my actions and behaviour left me with a guilt complex I still carry to this day.

The business had a Mini van and my pal, John Thomas (real name), would drive me to venues like London's Soho and Liverpool's Cavern Club to check out bands and act like a dynamic young impresario, with his brains in his trousers. The back of the van was filled with soft cushions and was also a useful accruement for my chosen path in life. When I was fully mobile with my own second-hand Ford Prefect 105 car I could take on the day-to-day duty of emptying the cash from the one-armed bandits and pinball machines. I had a special hand wound device to count the thousands of sixpenny pieces that generated the company cash flow, packing them into brown £5 bags.

The car also provided the means to get to the dance halls at night and meet more girls, including my wife Anne. She was different, shy and quiet, and became my Thursday night date. She was not the impulsive type, preferring to take time to make considered decisions, which was annoying. However, I was determined to win her over.

The business now expanded and had taken on an agency for a legal roulette gambling game called Legalite, which we placed in bingo halls and night clubs. It became a popular gambling game and was very lucrative, which allowed further expansion as the business took over the Dudley Hippodrome, a large theatre in Dudley situated next to the town's famous zoo. Legalite roulette changed the odds against the player as the zero, on the wheel, was the house number and if the ball dropped in that slot the entire bets placed on the table went to the house. The punter was also charged sixpence (two pence) for every bet, which the house kept as a betting fee. So in some ways this was familiar territory for a one-armed bandit player, each play costing sixpence.

It was a very different culture from dad's business though, requiring a team of attractive croupiers that had to be trained to run the tables. They were made up mostly of my aunties, from both sides of the family.

The Dudley Hippodrome used to be a great theatre and was still fully equipped but had fallen into decline, as so many had, not being able to make money from traditional live entertainment alone. So it was to become a Midlands Entertainment Agency bingo hall for five nights a week, with a purpose-built area at the rear of the stalls where two Legalite tables were installed and opened for playing during the break and for an hour after the bingo had finished.

Many of the Hippodrome staff had been there for a number of years and were pulled back in to act as front of house staff, bingo callers, bar staff and there was a uniformed commissionaire called Fred. The place was steeped in theatrical history, all recorded photographically in a small artist's bar under the stage called the Gluepot. The walls in this 'artists only' bar were adorned from floor to ceiling with autographed pictures of the stars that had appeared on the Hippodrome stage over the years. It was a veritable treasure trove of memorabilia that was eventually sadly lost. The Hippodrome had its own large annexe bar which I also christened the Gluepot, we ran dances featuring local live bands and it became a hotbed of action for the local pop adoring community. In the main theatre we put on wrestling bouts on a Sunday, which played to packed houses, with all of the icons of the day appearing, such as Mike Marino, Wayne Bridges, Docker Don Steadman and Billy Two Rivers. We held world championship fights for these exciting and well choreographed bouts, great entertainment. Although I wanted to do something special. One night stands!

It means something quite different today but in the sixties a *one night stand* meant bringing a big band to a gig for one night only. The first show I put on included Jerry Dorsey (now Engelbert Humperdinck) as the opening act. Then followed Pinkerton's Assorted Colours, who had charted with a Lennon and McCartney song and The Kinks, who were huge, to close the first half. The second half was taken up by a group from the USA who were massive in pop terms, The Walker Brothers. I bought the entire acts, for one night, two shows, for £1,000. There were thousands of kids outside with every ticket for the 1,700 seat auditorium sold for both shows. To generate extra revenue I would print three times the amount of programmes we needed with a number on each of them. We always sold out of the programmes. A lucky number was drawn, the recipient of which would go backstage to meet the stars. Only girls seemed to win it and always cute ones I wanted to get to know. The heating would be switched up to promote soft drink sales and with a full house I would generate £850 in profit, which was a great deal of money back then. I loved this side of the business and put on several shows, booking big time TV variety acts and rock bands. It really was the swinging sixties and I frequented all of the UK hot spots, mixing socially with all of the headliners of that period. It was a wonderful experience for a 17-year-old and I took full advantage of all the perks it offered.

There was a strange phenomenon happening at the Hippodrome. It concerned the theatre ghost. The staff, who had worked at the theatre for many years, would talk of Nora who died at the turn of the century, on stage, in suspicious circumstances. Nora often caused trouble, allegedly opening the secured front doors of the Hippodrome in the middle of the night. As I was the key holder I would be called out of my bed by the police at three o'clock in the morning to go and close them. I assumed that it was just customers hiding in the auditorium after the theatre had closed and I thought I had fixed this by chaining up all of the doors. It did not stop and I was called out every night for a week, getting to the Hippodrome to find one of the doors open with the padlock and chain undone! The staff told me it was just Nora and she would continue until she had got tired of it. I did not accept this and asked the security firm to place dogs in the theatre for the night. This had no effect either. The following night I was called by the police to go to the theatre. The doors had been opened and the dogs were wandering around Dudley High Street. Desperate to get a good night's sleep I coerced one of our door men, Billy Sargent, to stay in the theatre overnight. Billy was a big, tough guy and armed with a torch and a baseball bat he positioned himself in the middle of the stalls and waited. I still got the three o'clock in the morning call and arrived at the theatre to be met by Billy, in an agitated state. He told me he heard the chains rattling in one of the exit doors and ran to investigate. That door was still intact but now another chain was rattling in the dress circle exit. Billy made his way to those doors, the noise suddenly ceased but then he heard the chains rattling right at the top of the theatre, in the 'Gods' and finally back on the ground floor exit where he found the door open and the chains swinging. It nearly scared him to death and he flatly refused to do it again. As it turned out it was not necessary, the activity stopped, never to be repeated. Apparently Nora had won the day.

I was having a wonderful time and mixing with the music movers and shakers of the day. I attended the BBC Top of the Pops when the Beatles were performing. I recently recalled this event, John Lennon was using the F word, which my wife Anne (then girlfriend) did not appreciate. However, Anne recently informed me that she was not there so I don't know which girl I was with or whom John had offended. I was in there, right in the middle of this great period of British musical history and youth culture complete with snazzy suit, long hair and Cuban heeled boots, but it was all going to end and come crashing down around me.

My father's depression bouts were still frequent. He said the depression came down like a safety curtain at a theatre. Leaving him backstage, alone and in despair. I inherited some of those traits but have learned to control it. I read a book about Winston Churchill's depression which he referred to as 'the Black Dog' entering the room.

When it enters my room I try and take control of it by being its master. I tell it to 'sit down', 'stay' and 'shut the fuck up!' It works most of the time.

My father's mental health was deteriorating and at one point he went into a state of semi-consciousness for three days, unable to speak or eat and was admitted into a private mental hospital. He did not respond to treatment and despite all of his success, relative opulence and comfort he was admitted to Stafford Mental Hospital for a radical series of electric shock treatment. We were told that a strong electric current could shock the brain and hopefully reroute the brain's circuitry to displace the illogical and irrational thought process that was now in control. The process seemed to work for a while, I visited him regularly in that institution and began to comprehend the lack of understanding the medical profession had and, more importantly, the lack of solutions available to the unfortunate and lonely victims that endure mental health problems. I walked the wards of Stafford Mental Hospital looking at the confused, the lost and the insane and felt afraid for the future of my father.

He came home after a few weeks and life, for me, seemed good. Until Anne dumped me, as a result of my philandering after discovering I was in multiple relationships, including one with my cousin's wife. It was disgraceful. Not that I was any good at sex anyway. In fact I was hopeless at it. I had now developed an allergy to condoms which brought me out in a nasty rash. That was scary and I could not go to the clinic for sexually transmitted infections because the aforementioned Aunty Edna worked there. The doctor sorted it and I had to use special condoms made of sheep or pigs' bladder or stomach lining. They were not rubber and had to be held in place by a sort of bulldog clip, which hardly added to the occasion. I seem to recall they were called Triple X. At least they were biodegradable.

My mom had an inkling as to how I was conducting my life and hoped it would pass. My dad had no idea and would have been mortified. My mother stormed into my bedroom one morning, shook me awake and told me to get up quickly. I was awake instantly, out of bed and ready for the unknown crisis. I had been to see a girl in Macclesfield, some 50 miles north, arriving home at two o'clock in the morning. On the way back I had opened the window and disposed of the Triple X, in a typical irresponsible act of juvenile delinquency. Well, as I said, they were biodegradable. My mother now led me through the hallway, out of the front door and pointed at the car. To be more accurate, she pointed at the aerial on the back wing. Attached to it was the condom, waving gracefully in a light breeze like a mini wind sock.

'Get rid of that!' my mother hissed, adding, 'before your father gets up, you horrible little sod!'

Anne and I were back together in a couple of weeks, but during that spell apart I went completely on the rampage, met my first nymphomaniac, also called Ann, from West Bromwich and got myself ill. I was still 'operating' at the Hippodrome and had refined my girl pulling technique into a fine art. I would drive up to the Hippodrome steps, passing my car keys to the doorman Fred, for him to park the car, and I would then escort my girlfriend to a box from which to view the show. In my box was a drinks trolley with my favourite tipple on it, brandy with lime juice. I drank a lot in those days.

The MC (Master of Ceremonies) for all of our shows was a chap called Paul Short, he would always open the show with the words, 'Ladies and gentlemen, welcome to another night of entertainment from the Midlands Entertainment Agency. Tonight Mr Mike is escorting the lovely miss . . . (whoever I was with at the time), so please welcome her to the Hippodrome.' At that point the spotlight would go to the box and my lady of the evening would wave gracefully at the auditorium, soaking up the adoration. Except for Anne, she would dive down, ducking below the rim of the box, horrified by the embarrassment of the applause and the odd ribald comment from the stalls the likes of 'go on Mick, give her one'.

I was drinking far too much and I was to go to sleep one night and not wake up for three days. I was at times delirious and my mother said I was talking in a semi-conscious stupor about Anne. Which Anne I did not know but I hoped it was not Ann from West Bromwich. When I woke up Anne was sitting by my bedside, my mother having called her as it appeared I was asking for her in my sleep. Bugger! When I woke up and saw Anne I realised that I was in love with this girl. So after four years of my debauched and reprehensible behaviour we got married and moved into a small bungalow. My father paid a deposit of £750, as a wedding present, and a mortgage company supplied the rest of the money.

We had some wonderful times on dad's 40 foot canal cruiser and life seemed idyllic, apart from dad's ongoing and often violent bouts of depression. Dad had finally tracked down his father and my sister and he went to Ireland to meet him, 40 years after he had deserted the family home. They learned at this first meeting that the woman he had run away with had passed away, but he had recently remarried. Unfortunately, my grandmother was still alive so this meant he was now a bigamist, for the second time, and the original plan of bringing him back to the UK was a non-starter.

Grandfather's latest wife, Peggy, knew nothing of her bigamous husband's past – as far as she was concerned she had married Maurice Edwards – the surname Kendrick having been deliberately dropped. So a story was woven about my real grandfather being an old family friend and we were all to refer to him as Maurice Edwards, in order to keep this dark secret from her.

Maurice and Peggy were brought to England on occasions but we had to be careful, none of dad's sisters could know of this arrangement since they all hated their father for what he had done to the family. Although I was glad dad had found this missing piece in his life. He had wanted to find his father, but I don't know if it helped repair all of the emotional damage.

Eventfully Maurice died and dad recalled going to the funeral in Dublin. Although he had been reunited with his father he realised that his relationship had been shallow. He sat, by himself, at the back of the church, unacknowledged by the family. He felt alone and deserted again.

Peggy sent Maurice's war medals to the British Legion, explaining that she wanted them to keep them. He was an undoubtedly a courageous man, having been cited for bravery during World War I, rescuing some injured comrades under fire. His diary stated, 'Jerry were a running but I was a running faster.' The Legion wrote back to her saying that the medals were not awarded to Maurice Edwards but to a Maurice Edward Kendrick. Peggy immediately made the call to my dad.

* * *

We did continue to have some wonderful times as our children came along, Myles, then James, and we spent many happy weekends at the coast in North Wales where dad now had a house on the harbour quay and a 32 foot motorboat moored in the bay.

Although things were to change as the dark clouds of financial hardship were looming. Several of the gaming laws had changed and revenues were dropping. Dad's mental health plummeted again and he was inconsolable and uncontrollable. His main topic of conversation was of ending it all and he obviously required constant watching and attention while on a regime of tranquilisers and other drugs, of which he regularly took too many. My mother had suffered her own nervous breakdown and also spent time in Stafford Mental Hospital, she really did not have the strength of mind to handle the situation.

The doctor was called and in a self-induced drug stupor dad was sectioned under the mental health act, for his own safety. It was a horrible gut wrenching decision that affected us badly and I had to take calls from him over the next few weeks with him pleading and begging to get him out of there. When he did finally come home he was fit enough to understand that the business was going nowhere, but it was to get worse. Much, much worse.

Harold Wilson's Labour government came into power and restructured some of the UK's corporate and personal tax laws, backdating some of them, and we faced a tax bill of £70,000. That was an enormous amount of money at that time but my father refused to file for bankruptcy, fearing the shame it would bring. Somehow he found the money.

In those days income tax was very high, with some individuals paying up to 97p in the pound. It was a punitive rate that did not incentivise the entrepreneur and drove away growth and investment while encouraging a culture of 'under the bed money' that was siphoned away for a rainy day. Most people knew the adverse effect of this type of taxation, a so-called 'Brain Drain' had started with the higher paid executives and academics leaving these shores for overseas postings. Here they found a fairer, more liberal governing authority, which better understood that a policy to motivate ambition and generate wealth for those individuals was the key driver in establishing long term sustainability of the economies. High taxation inhibits growth and suppresses the desire of individuals to do well and improve their position in life. What is the point?

So, dad found the £70,000 in cash which cleaned him out. The problem was he was then taxed on that undeclared money and incurred penalties and, somehow, had to raise another £35,000. That ruined him. Everything had to go, the boats, the cars, the house and the jobs, including mine.

I was still young but there was very little call for an ex one-arm bandit mechanic. I had to get a job. I was a resilient young man. I had come from a poorish family that got rich and placed a silver spoon in my mouth. It had been a great ride until that spoon had been yanked out and I needed to find a new career. I tried one or two jobs, selling collating machines, then ladders and, quite successfully, fork lift trucks. I finally talked my way into an advertising agency in Birmingham, eventually starting a PR division, the function and activity of which I confess I knew absolutely nothing about.

I was close to my father and spoke to him on a daily basis. It was a relationship that went past simply being his eldest son. He needed me and told me so, often. I gave all I could give to help him and my mother, during the dark days, as any son would. I had an arrangement that when the 'black dog' appeared or the safety curtain came down, he was to call me instantly. My parents again tried faith healing, visiting several spiritual churches in the area, and Anne and I accompanied them on occasions to the meetings. On the whole they were generally happy events, with much singing and talking to 'spirits' through mediums for guidance and advice. I have to say it had positive affects on some people. I have seen people confined to wheelchairs jumping up and ballet dancing in the aisles, unknown illnesses disappear and feelings of well-being thrust upon the eager congregation. Some of the mediums would assume the voice of the 'spirit' that was leading them and put members of the congregation in touch with departed loved ones, validating the messages by informing them of incidents known only to them.

My wife Anne had been suffering from a rash on her skin for three years which the doctors and medical specialists had been unable to cure. My mother asked a healer to look at it. I remember a white-haired gentleman with intense blue eyes staring at her. It made her cry.

He just held her hand and said, 'It will go now.' And, most miraculously, it did. He then turned to me and said, 'Please stop asking your wife, "what's the matter?" over and over again.' Anne started to cry silently again, not having spoken a word during the entire process. I was stunned. How did he know that? Anne had been suffering from the 'baby blues' post natal depression and I was driving her mad with the insensitive and repetitive question.

There is no doubt that this type of spiritual church helped a lot of people. Whether it is a person's search for answers that seem otherwise unavailable which instil a self-belief, a sort of mentally placed placebo, or is purely coincidental, I don't know. But it did not help my dad. I spent hours on the phone at all times of the day, sometimes until the early hours of the morning, reassuring him, comforting him, motivating him, trying to get back to that big personality that could move mountains, have fun and inspire people. He tried everything but it all seemed to come to nothing. He felt a failure.

My wife and I went on holiday to Cornwall with friends. Mobile phones were still some years away. He could not talk to me. He drove to a pub car park, dissolved 200 paracetamol in water and drank it, drove back home to my mother and died in front of her, aged 59. Amen. I was devastated, felt lost, bitter and guilty.

Someone once told me that when you lose someone close you are often told that, in time, you will get over it. They added that I should never try to get over it, but I should try to get used to it. That helped me a lot. I have never got over losing my dad and still carry that loss today – but I did get used to it.

Chapter Four

An Idiot Abroad

The Dudley Zoo General Manager John Shields had mentioned to me that he was off to Zambia to take a look at the Red Lechwe, deer that moved in herds across the African plains and which were diminishing in numbers. He wanted to consider the possibility of buying a breeding pair of these beautiful animals.

In the meantime, the balloon pilot John Gore had discussed that the current world altitude record for balloons was easily breakable and we should look for a sponsor. We discussed the details of this and it greatly appealed to me. It was a journey that would later influence my future and threaten my life.

I informed John Shields about this altitude record attempt and decided to join him on his trip to Zambia to consider Africa as the ideal continent in which to undertake such a challenge. I knew next to nothing about the complexities involved in a project like this but suggested that I accompany him on the journey on a fact finding mission. The curator was well up for it and we climbed onto a Boeing 727 bound for Lusaka, on a Zambia airlines flight from Heathrow. It was a journey that would shape my ballooning future and begin my love affair with the African continent.

For some time Zambia had been unstable, until politician Kenneth Kaunda, or KK as he was affectionately known, had led the country to independence in 1964. The UNIP had won a major election, defeating their ANC rivals and securing Kaunda's position as Prime Minister. Although financially Zambia was still a poor country, politically it was now stable.

Our trip to Zambia was aboard the London Heathrow to Lusaka inaugural flight and there were a great number of journalists on board. John Shields and I were quick to seize the opportunity to tell them about the balloon and handed out press releases and a picture of Thursday's Child, with its new branding advertising Dudley Zoo. I was approached by a Mr Raphael who wrote for the Financial Times and was also a reporter for some major African newspapers. He wrote the story on the flight and obviously filed it soon after we arrived in Lusaka. Zambia is a fascinating country and Lusaka a sophisticated capital, in African terms anyway.

Despite Zambia's sophistication and level of appreciation of the Western style development, it was still intrinsically African and Third World. Understandably, they had no idea of what a hot air balloon was, what they looked like or how they worked. The story written about my visit and my intentions appeared on the front page of the Zambian Times but the picture was printed upside down, with the basket at the top. 'Why don't you fall out?' was the most frequent question I was asked, along with 'Where are the engines?' and 'How does it fly?'

The most amusing interview was with Zambian Radio. The interviewer had a list of questions that he was determined to get through, irrespective of my answers.

'Mr Mike,' said the interviewer, looking at the Zambia Times photograph. 'I see a big balloon and a basket that you are bringing to Zambia. Why don't you fall out – are you tied in?'

'No,' I replied, 'that photograph is upside down. The pilot stands in the basket with the balloon above them. There is a burner in the basket that creates hot air. This makes the balloon hot and, as hot air rises, the balloon lifts off the ground. The balloon can go to great heights and we are bringing it to Zambia to break the world altitude record.'

'So, Mr Mike,' continued the interviewer, 'I believe the balloon has no engines, so, tell me, how does it fly in the air and what are you bringing this balloon to Zambia for?'

'As I said,' I offered, taking a deep breath, 'it rises because it is a hot air balloon. The balloon holds the hot air and as hot air is lighter than cold air, it rises above the ground. We want to capture the world altitude record and as Zambia is a country offering fine and stable wind conditions, it is a good place to launch. And we think we could get to a height of 55,000 feet.' I finished off, desperately looking for the words to make this comprehensible, wondering if any listeners were still tuned in.

'I see,' said the interviewer. 'And how high do you think you could get and why is Zambia a good place to do this?'

And so it went on, but I was not the only interviewee subject to this penetrating journalistic treatment. There was an equestrian team in Lusaka at the time.

'Good afternoon madam, can you tell our listeners why you have arrived in Lusaka?'

'Good afternoon. We are a British equestrian team and have come here to compete in the Zambian dressage event being held in Lusaka and we have brought a team of six riders and horses.'

'How many riders and horses have you brought to Zambia and what will they all be doing here?'

In fairness this radio station was a new venture in Zambia and they were doing a great job breaking into fresh skill sets. The station was managed by a British ex-patriot and he had taken a pragmatic view of rolling with it and was enjoying the entire experience. The alternative was letting it drive you completely insane.

He told me that he had met the weather forecaster in a hallway the previous week, just before he was about to broadcast the weather forecast. The manager informally asked the presenter what the situation was for the one minute slot that he was about to report on and he told him, 'It's easy today, Boss, I will tell them that I have just been on the roof and it am pissing down.'

I just love Africa, I really do.

However, there was some serious business to attend to. We needed to get permission from just about every Ministry; Aviation, Agriculture, Wildlife, Tourism and a host of other permits from the Military Police. The list went on and on.

One of the big concerns came from the Wildlife department. They did not want us scaring the animals or setting fire to the bushlands, putting the animals in jeopardy. They were also concerned about the crew's safety. They were aware that a project like this would create international comment and wanted to make sure that Zambia was well thought of. In particular they were keen to make quite sure that the balloon crew and attending media were all kept safe. There had been a recent fatality with Anglia, a British television company making a wildlife film for a series called Horizon. An elephant had charged at the camera and the operator, a lady by the name of Penny, had been killed. Looking through a camera lens can give a false perspective and she did not realise the close proximity of the charging animal. It ran right through the camera and killed her.

We were assigned a group of four wildlife guides and trackers that were going to take us deep into the bush to familiarise us with the area and its animal occupants.

'Mr Mike,' they said, 'if an elephant or rhino charge towards you, you must run away or they will kill you. But if a lion chases you, you must stand still. If you run away, it will chase you and kill you, very quick, and eat you. Some lions are very clever and will follow you along a track then go in front of you and wait. When you get to them they will jump on you and kill you. So if a lion comes to you, you must stand up straight, with your arms in the air and shout and shout . . . 'AAAAHHHH!' very loud.

I had no problem at all with shouting 'AAAAHHHH!' very loud in those circumstances. My plan, if I landed in the bush, would be to put the balloon basket in the upright position and turn on the burners if any unwanted attention came my way.

Actually my biggest worry was snakes, spiders and other creepy crawlies. I had a terrible phobia about those critters. The Zambian group were most amused with my reticence to go near spiders or snakes. They would point at spiders and tell me which ones were very bad and pick up those that were harmless, waving them too close to me. 'Mr Mike, this one is OK, not poisonous. That one there is very bad. 30 seconds and you are dead.' They would then stamp on it furiously.

They were very brave with snakes. 'This am a green mamba and will kill you slowly.' They would catch it with their hands, grasping it behind the head, its mouth open, displaying ugly venomous fangs. They would cut off its head and bury it deep enough to make sure that it was safe and no one could tread on it. 'That one is a python,' they would point out and say, 'it can make a bad bite which will not kill you but they will wrap around you, squeeze you until you are dead and eat you whole.' They were very matter of fact about the whole process. I, on the other hand, was terrified, and constantly searched my immediate vicinity for anything with scales or more legs than me!

I have never liked spiders and snakes and at Dudley Zoo and I always gave the reptile house a wide berth. The keepers would feed the snakes baby chicks which pecked playfully around the enclosure to the 'umms' and 'aahhs' of the visitors who would then be horrified, and probably damaged for life, as they witnessed the predators strike like lightning and have them for lunch. It was not good for business and the zoo changed the protocol by having the chicks euthanized, frozen and fed outside of visiting hours.

So the Zambian wildlife guides thought it was most amusing that this man from England would fly one of those balloon things, yet was scared senseless of insects, bugs and snakes.

We were lucky to witness a rare but rather sad sight one day. A lioness was trying to kill an isolated antelope. It was crazed with fear as the lioness chased it down. The buck ran wildly, blind with fear and banging into trees in panic, but the big cat could not get to her. We watched, absorbed, as the two animals fought their own battles for survival, one intent on eating and the other in not being eaten. They ran in circles while moving closer to our position. It became apparent that the lioness was injured, her front left leg was not operating correctly, which was the reason she could not catch the buck easily. The guides were jabbering away, excitedly, in their own language and went into English to tell us that the lioness, because of her injury, was hungry and desperate for food and they added that we had better leave the area.

However, it was obvious that the big cat was getting too close. Far too close. She stopped, looked at us and bounded towards us very quickly, if in an ungainly manner with an awkward gait.

We were transfixed, unable to move as the animal covered the ground in seconds, despite her lame left leg. I remembered what they had said about lions, 'stand up, make yourself big and shout AAAAHHHH!' I was scared senseless and could not move anyway while the guides, steeped in knowledge and experience, had run off shouting 'shit' in Swahili leaving us standing there. The cat dropped in exhaustion at our feet, well my feet, and part of her body was pinning my foot to the ground. The guides, who had taken refuge and were now assembled behind some nearby rocks, began shouting instructions but I realised that we were in no danger. The cat was exhausted, lying half on her side with her huge tongue hanging from her mouth. I bent down to remove my foot from underneath her.

'Mr Mike, don't go near her mouth,' they shouted. But she was not able to do anything. As I bent down the lioness was looking at me, breathing heavily, and did not move as I extracted my shoe. I was wearing safari type 'Hush Puppy' boots and I can inform you that it stuck to lion fur like Velcro. It was quite difficult to extract myself. We left the animal there and I was hoping that they would go back and shoot her, but they explained that this was the way of the bush and they would leave it to sort itself out in the natural way. I argued that it was kinder to shoot her but they smiled with a look that implied that I had no idea what I was talking about. And they were right. It was all a great learning experience for me. I was a complete novice and didn't have any idea of what I was taking about. Although I would learn fast and, in time, would question and challenge many of the tenets of

African culture, and society, where I felt it would benefit the continent and its people.

A stunning and desperately sad example of how African people had to run their lives was demonstrated to me the following day. We were on a two hour drive into the bush to see the Minister of Agriculture. On the way, along a dirt road, we came across a terrible car accident. Only one car was involved, an ageing light green Austin Cambridge that had obviously rolled over and most of the body panels were badly distorted, including the roof. A few local villagers stood around the car, which was a total wreck, and with a natural curiosity and an obvious desire to help, we pulled up alongside. There were two people in the car and it was immediately apparent that they had not survived the crash. It was a sickening and heart wrenching sight and the hopelessness of the situation affected me instantly and permanently. My driver was anxious to get us away from there and seemed to have a fatalistic view, accepting the inevitability of it all. Death is no stranger to many Africans.

We drove on to the Ministry building and presented ourselves to the receptionist who asked us to take a seat and wait. Waiting for ministers was par for the course and I was to get used to it over the years. After forty minutes, we were not asked into his office; instead the Minister came to the reception area to meet us. He looked a serious and intense man as he moved forward to meet us and shake our hands, saying, 'Have you come from Lusaka?'

'Yes, we have, your Excellency,' I replied. He then explained that his wife had just been killed in a car accident and asked if we would be good enough to take him back to the capital, as he had released his driver for the day.

Our immediate reaction was one of condolence and sadness for this man and we instinctively knew that the crash we had witnessed was the accident in question. Worse still, we were about to drive past it again with the Minister in the car. It really was one of those situations when I had no idea what to say or how to behave. We did not say a lot and drove back towards Lusaka. As we approached the crash scene I saw that the car was now just an empty shell. In less than two hours most of it had gone and the victims removed. The wheels and tyres had been taken off, all of the seats had gone and the bonnet was raised so I presumed that the useable engine parts had been removed.

We drove past in complete silence, not a word from the Minister or ourselves. What was there to say? Life and death in Africa is met with a level of acceptance that can be difficult for us to understand. They are no less saddened than we are at the loss of a loved one and can be loud and verbose in the demonstration of that sadness, particularly when a child is lost. In my view, hundreds of years of subservience, suppression and deprivation have left them with a realisation of the futility of that emotion. Through the ages they have needed to accept the hand that is dealt them and get on with it, with the help of the family unit and an absolute and undoubting faith in their God.

The Minster got out of the car in Lusaka, nodded to us, and went to bury his wife.

We surveyed several bush areas by light aircraft owned by an ex-military type, now a businessman, who lived in Lusaka. He was not happy with the way things were moving forward in Africa. Independence in Zambia was now established and he thought the black population was becoming too powerful, a throwback to colonialism. A typical brusque, outspoken individual with an arrogant view that 'The Blacks' were getting above themselves. I remember walking down a street in Lusaka with him and his wife where a group of locals were sitting on the pavement blocking the path. It was just a social gathering. His wife looked at the group and suggested that we should walk around them. 'No,' he said, placing a swagger stick he always carried under his right armpit. 'We'll walk right through 'em,' and he marched on scattering the young locals.

He took us in his aircraft into the bush the following day and we landed on a dirt strip to visit a tribal chief. When we returned to the plane he drained some of the fuel into a glass jar to examine it. When I enquired what he was doing he explained, 'Standard pre take off procedure, old chap. Just checking the buggers haven't put sand in the fuel in an effort to kill me.' Now why would they want to do that, I thought sarcastically?

Before we left Zambia, we had a big party in a town called Mazabuka, west of the capital. It became a huge drinking contest with the Zambian white fraternity determined to drink the Brits under the table. They lost.

The drinking stopped for a short period when someone raised the alarm. There was a child on the clubhouse lawn with a snake wrapped around her leg. She was still in nappies so was no more than a toddler. Her father was very calm about it, although you can imagine the undeniable danger of her being bitten and the effects on her young body trying to deal with the lethal injection of snake venom. He simply picked up the child and the snake uncoiled itself from her leg while another man pinned the reptile to the grass with a garden rake and killed it. I don't know how I would have handled that situation. As far as Africa was concerned I was still as green as the grass upon which that snake was killed. The opportunity for embarrassment in unknown territories is high and I was to learn that, in Kenya, on my next visit to the Dark Continent.

It came when I learned that balloons were flying in the Masai Mara, over the Serengeti. The large game reserve, Masai Mara National Reserve, sits next to the Serengeti National Park in Tanzania and stretches into Kenya. The Serengeti is globally famous for its huge population of lions, leopards and cheetahs. The highlight for many is the annual migration of wildebeest, Thomson's gazelle and of course zebra. This spectacular event, to and from the Serengeti, happens every year from July to October, and is known as the Great Migration.

The famous explorer and filmmaker Alan Root had taken a balloon to the area as a camera platform for one of his fine films. I can still remember a sequence from the balloon when they filmed the slow moving shadow of the balloon moving over a heard of wildebeest. The animals moved away, without panicking, as the shadow moved up to them, probably a deep primeval instinct alerting them to the unnaturalness of it all. Some entrepreneurial balloon pilots had started balloon flights for tourists over the Masai Mara in Kenya and I wanted to explore the possibilities.

Dick Wirth of Thunder Balloons had built balloons for this purpose and advised me of how to get there and who to ask for. I arrived in Nairobi and, after spending a night at the famous Norfolk Hotel, I made my way to Wilson Airport to hire a small twin engine aircraft to fly me to the Masai Mara. The flight gave me a chance to understand the vastness of the African plains and the Great Rift Valley, with its abundance of wildlife and home to a variety of colourful and cultured tribes. The plan was to visit Governors' Camp, a small collection of grass huts, nestling on the banks of the Mara River, built for the tourists to sleep in and a lodge where visitors would eat, drink and watch the sunset after their game drive. It was paradise personified.

The aircraft approach procedure was well set out. The pilot of the twin Navaho aircraft would radio the camp fifteen minutes before we were to arrive, he would land on the grass airstrip and the camp truck would pick me up and transport me to the lodge.

I watched the pilot line up for the runway and then perform a low pass to clear away the odd zebra and antelope grazing on the short grass landing strip before turning the aircraft around and finally touching down. He explained that he would drop me off here and then wait until the truck arrived, just to make sure I would be OK. He would then taxi off to the end of the runway to make take off into the wind. I told him not to bother hanging around, I would just get off and wait for them. 'I will be fine,' I explained, with a nodding, 'I've done it all before' smirk. I also added that it was windy with some cloud so the hot sun would not be a problem.

I got out of the door and he told me he was not thinking about the sun, but this was lion country. I gulped quickly and for some reason told him I would still be ok. After all, I thought to myself, I knew Africa and I was wearing a safari suit jacket and bush hat, proper boots and everything. I thought I looked cool. Looking back, I think he thought I was a total dickhead.

I watched him taxi to the end of the runway and take off waving at me as he lifted off. I stood there about 50 yards from the white 20 foot tall pole to which was attached a wind sock. I did a full 360 degree circle look around with check list. Right . . . antelope, zebra, giraffe, ostrich, lion. Lion! Shit, lion! I could see the telling patches of brown on the animal's ears that identified it as a lioness as she lay low in the tall grass on the edge of the landing strip. I had no weapon and I needed to get to a safe position. I thought of the windsock pole. Perhaps I could shimmy up that if she came to attack me. I quietly walked towards the pole checking on the position of the lioness every few yards. She was following me. Although it was very windy I was getting very hot and sweaty. I removed my camera from around my neck, reasoning that it was a heavy weight on a strap. If the lion came for me I could swing it around my head and bounce it off her skull. I got to the windsock pole and waited and the thought occurred to me that if I went up the pole, she would be able to climb it more easily than I. As I waited in a very nervous, hot and sweaty state I reckoned that the camera was the best bet. At that moment there was a loud roar behind me and I turned round instantly shouting, 'AAAAHHHH' and swinging the camera around my head, terrified. The actual 'roar' noise was the klaxon horn on a Toyota land cruiser in which sat Winston, the now wide-eyed guide from the lodge. I ran up to the cruiser and quickly jumped in.

'Are you Mr Mike?' he said, staring intently at me.

'Yes,' I said and pointed, 'Simba!' I shouted. 'Simba!' You see, I was so well travelled, I even knew the name for lion in the local language.

'No Simba here, Mr Mike, no Simba here,' said Winston. But I knew what I had seen and pointed frantically at the spot where the lioness was lying in wait for me. 'No Simba, Mr Mike,' Winston repeated and drove slowly towards the spot that revealed a large oblong heap with two lioness ear shaped peaks. 'Termite mound, Mr Mike. No Simba,' said Winston with a huge grin on his face and a knowing look in his eyes that said, 'you stupid English twat'. I still think it followed me down the runway.

I spent a few days in Governors' Camp and every time I saw Winston with his mates I could hear them giggling and whispering 'Simba'. On one occasion one of them was rocking with laughter while making a circular motion with his hand over his head – obviously mimicking my swinging of the camera – they all seemed to have a great sense of humour.

The local Government had just issued three new balloon licenses so I decided that it would be too crowded and that I needed to find a new market for passenger balloons in Africa. I would go take a look at Tanzania. Although back at the office a new and exciting African adventure was beginning to materialise.

Chapter Five

That's the Wonder of Woolworths

I had seen the press potential of balloons after flying Thursday's Child around Shropshire and felt that there must be a place for commercial airships some time in the near future. For my company, Lighter Than Air Ltd, I designed a simple black and white logo comprising a simple outline of a hot air balloon in the middle of one of an airship. I had also seen a photograph of a hot air airship in the USA with the Budweiser logos placed on it but learned that it was not successful. However, other balloonists were now getting involved and an old Etonian chap called Colin Prescott had started a company called The Hot Air Balloon Company. We were to become bitter rivals over the years, finally becoming partners, some time later, in another related business.

I went into full PR pitch mode and contacted candidate companies with the proposition that they sponsor a balloon, successfully arranging a meeting with the F W Woolworth management team. Woolworths would buy the balloon, although it would belong to Lighter Than Air Ltd who would operate it on their behalf. They would pay a daily flying fee and the balloon would be flown at store openings, agricultural shows and other events with large public gatherings, creating a lot of positive press comment. To my astonishment this famously conservative company agreed. Lighter Than Air Ltd was up and running.

Luckily, I was self-employed at the time. My Birmingham PR company had merged with a larger concern called Good Relations Ltd. We had taken the business into a public company and I resigned, just before the point that I would have been sacked. So starting my own public relations consultancy was an easy decision to make and I retained my shareholding in the company which I subsequently sold back to Good Relations Ltd, but took most of my clients with me to open a new PR company in Wolverhampton. I could now concentrate on the Lighter Than Air Ltd business and had two great clients; Dudley Zoo and Woolworths.

Unfortunately it became apparent that what I was doing was technically illegal. A Board of Trade regulation prohibited aerial advertising. I argued that if BOAC (now British Airways) could put its name on an aircraft then so could we. The Board of Trade advised me that I could put the name of the charterer or hirer on the balloons but no slogans. So I formed a company, with Woolies' permission, called 'That's the Wonder of Woolworths Ltd', which neatly circumvented the regulations. During those times I won other contracts and became MD of a company called Milk's Gotta Lotta Bottle Ltd, for the Milk Marketing Board, Nivea – Out Of The Blue Ltd and many others.

I was just applying for the name 'Everest Double Glazing, call 0121-0456-789 for a Free Brochure – No Representative Will Call Ltd', when the Board of Trade gave up arguing with me. The law changed and we were officially allowed to advertise.

I commissioned the Woolworths balloon with Thunder Balloons Ltd. It was to be a 77,000 cubic feet, red balloon, with the logo emblazoned in white and all the bells and whistles you could wish for. It included aluminium fuel flight cylinders (much lighter than the steel ones in Thursday's Child) and complete with an instrument pack consisting of an altimeter, variometer (which indicated how fast you were rising or falling) and a thermometer which told you how hot the balloon was getting at the crown. The thermometer was an important instrument since you could overheat the balloon to past the melting point of the fabric. Up until then balloons had a heat flag at the top of the envelope that featured a soldered link which melted if it got too hot and fluttered down into the basket indicating that you had overheated the balloon. It was disconcerting for the heat flag to drop into the basket, just as you were taking off which it often did, but you were on the way up and could do absolutely nothing about it. Overheating the envelope was something you needed to avoid. It degraded the fabric and weakened it considerably. If the fabric became very hot it would simply melt and large holes would appear which released the hot air that was keeping the balloon aloft.

Around this time, balloon meets or rallies were starting to spring up, including the Bristol Balloon Fiesta in August and the Icicle meet in Newbury in January. At these meets, particularly the Icicle meet, brave pilots, flying in cold winter weather, would often make bravado statements like 'it's very windy so I'll fly solo', indicating that it was too dangerous to risk passengers. But being slightly daring and eccentric they were prepared to risk their own lives. It was very funny to listen to and watch.

There were more balloons appearing and a growing demand for them at shows and public gatherings of all descriptions, for which the organisers were willing to pay. At a £100 per day it was good money and all of our weekends were normally booked during the summer. Of course, I was still under training so had to pay for a qualified pilot for every event so it was onwards and upwards to my check out flight.

I flew every weather slot possible, some flights personifying absolute peace and tranquillity with soft landings in light and variable winds with easy access for the chase crew. On the other hand, there were some flights in fast winds, with bone breaking landings that involved carrying the equipment out of an often muddy field, piece by piece. At the same time I continued swatting for the theoretical exams, which I subsequently passed.

The Woolworths balloon was delivered in a large white van by the Thunder Balloons boss, Dick Wirth, to the Weston Park estate near Wolverhampton. We were all waiting with great excitement, dressed in our new 'Woolworths Balloon Crew' liveried flying jackets and crash helmets. Helmets were beginning to become accepted in ballooning circles as a sensible addition to flying apparel.

Weston Park is the ancestral seat of the Earls of Bradford and home of the current Earl, Richard Bridgeman, and his family. They were very pleased to have our balloon at the estate as ballooning is, after all, an outdoor pursuit and generated interest for their numerous visitors. My first visit to the park was during a training flight when Thursday's Child had taken me over the estate and I had landed in the parkland, between the great Sequoia redwood trees that seem to be a feature of many of the ancestral homes in the UK. I recall flying over a lake to look for a landing spot when two geese, startled by the burners, took flight and flew down wind below us. There was a sudden bang and they fell out of the sky on to the shore where two men with shotguns appeared. I shouted, 'Sorry,' to the men below and they shouted back, 'That was great, thank you.' They were obviously not angry, on the contrary, and I was confused. I didn't know if I should feel guilty for sending these birds to their death or pleased that I had helped these men in the pursuit of their hunting activity.

In any event, I decided to land and accomplished this with the normal and acceptable bump and drag. Lord Bradford appeared in a Land Rover with the obligatory black Labrador and was rather pleased to see us, not fazed at all by the basket wide drag mark we had left on his beautifully manicured parkland. He, like most people that encountered a hot air balloon and its occupants for the first time, asked us how we had got there, where we had come from, how high we had flown, was it cold up there – while admonishing the dog, several times, for piddling up the basket.

I explained to his Lordship that we had a chase crew looking for us and that it was standard practice for them to contact the landowner to get permission to retrieve the balloon before they drove on to his land. I further explained that the crew did not know where we were and I needed to call a retrieve number to give them our coordinates.

'Well, you had better come up to the house and call them,' he offered helpfully and he drove me to the front door of Weston Park, a magnificent country house set in more than a 1,000 acres of beautiful landscaped parkland.

I removed my very muddy boots and walked into the beautiful entrance hall of this grand house that had received so many historical guests during its history and was directed to the telephone. It was a black, dial type instrument, with a small padlock on. Lord Bradford unlocked the padlock and I called the crew, replacing the receiver, handing 2p to his Lordship for the call, which he accepted.

Lord Bradford made it quite plain that we could land on his estate any time and I asked him if we could use the estate as a take off point, some time in the future, when the wind was from a favourable direction, a question that he enthusiastically answered in the affirmative.

We had arranged delivery of the Woolworths balloon to Weston Park since the wind was forecast as coming from an easterly direction, taking us away from Wolverhampton and Birmingham. Dick Wirth was to make a delivery flight with us since the new balloon had a 'parachute rip' which neither Tony Gough nor I had any experience with. Like so many planned flights, the weather turned out not to be suitable and we had to be content with an oral brief from Dick on how to operate the parachute rip; preflight, in-flight and on landing. Before he left he suggested that we try and find a pilot with parachute rip experience for our first flight as they were great but could be vicious if not used properly. However, we couldn't wait could we?

We were back at Patshull Park, this time as far away from the lake as we could get. I inflated Woolworths and we had no problem setting the parachute rip. The rip is set in place, for the inflation, by small Velcro tabs. Once inflated you release the rip from the tabs, with the rip line, it settles back into the top of the envelope and we were ready to go. Tony was the pilot in charge and it was Rob Jones' turn for a flight. Tony instructed the ground crew 'weight off the basket' and we rose gently into the air in my brand new, pristine, big red balloon, in a wind of about 5 to 8 knots. Tony made a couple of test 'dumps' with the parachute rip (the process of letting the hot air out on the top of the envelope) while the balloon was climbing through to 1,000 feet. All seemed well. The dump arrested the ascent of the balloon quite quickly and the parachute snapped back into place. It seemed perfectly manageable. Rob Jones took the burner for some practice and we ambled about the sky enjoying ourselves.

We could see the chase crew below and Tony decided to land in a downwind field that had tall coniferous trees along the approaching perimeter. This scenario is always a favoured choice as the trees shield some of the ground wind as you dip down behind them, making the landing more comfortable. The procedure was to just clip the tops of the trees as you passed over them and dump the balloon straight into the field, in the shelter of those trees. That was the theory anyway. What actually happened on this occasion was somewhat different. The balloon hit the trees about 20 feet down and the envelope leant over, bending the tree severely, tipping the basket over and leaving Tony, Rob and I staring directly at the ground. We held on for grim death, trying to avoid being tipped out of the basket, which was on its side 40 feet up the tree.

Rob was in the front swearing violently, his torso half out of the basket. We all thought that the envelope would right itself naturally and lift the balloon off the tree in a few seconds, or the basket would force itself through the tree and on to the field. None of that happened. As the envelope started to rise the basket became weightless for a split second and the tree trunk violently flicked the basket into the air. In my mind's eye I can still see Rob's body completely outside of the basket, his legs in the air and his hands gripping the rope handles fiercely. The envelope was now above us, but with little air in it. Tony applied the burners which burnt through the mouth of my new balloon, but it was too late. We catapulted into the air and slammed into the hard ground with a sickening thud. Rob crawled out of the basket first and was articulate and verbose in his condemnation of balloons.

'I'm sick of these bloody things, every time I get into an effing balloon,' he went on, 'it tries to effing kill me. I thought these new effing parachute rips were supposed to give you a good landing. I think my effing back's broken.'

∗ ∗ ∗

I just had to get more practice. My check out flight had been sched-uled and with none other than the CAA examiner, the legend that was Wingco (Wing Commander) Jerry Turnbull.

Reportedly the Wingco was a nice old chap and I was advised that he was a fair but difficult taskmaster and that he did not charge a fee, per se, but would accept a duck supper at his favourite restaurant. It was also whispered to me that, as he was getting on now, he preferred to do check outs from a showground, nod, nod, wink, wink. In other words, he was booked to appear at a showground and put on a balloon demonstration and flight, for which he was paid. I would turn up for the test effectively doing his display for him. I thought that was rather clever and I had no problem with it.

Normally the terms and conditions on a balloon show attendance were that only 50 per cent of the fee would be paid if a flight was not pos-sible due to inclement weather. Fine, I reasoned, no problem with that. I called him to request a check out flight and, true to form, he simply and curtly informed me my check out was scheduled for May 18 (1977) from the Nuneaton Show at 1800 hours. Before he put the phone down he added, 'and I will expect you to demonstrate the use of a trail rope.'

Trail rope? What's a trail rope? Well Thursday's Child had a trail rope but I had never used it and neither had any of the pilots I had known or trained with. Basically, it was a 100 feet long and two inches thick piece of rope that was rolled into a ball of about 18 inches diameter and weighted 50 lbs. The theory was to throw it out at one hundred feet, just before landing. As the balloon descended the weight of the rope would decrease, making the landing softer and, the drag across the field shorter.

I had no time to practice, as no flying weather slot had presented itself, so I took the Woollies balloon, with my crew, to the Nuneaton show. Anyway, I reasoned, a trail rope is old fashioned and the new parachute rips made them redundant. When the Wing Commander saw it was a new Thunder 77 balloon he would realise it was not necessary, would he not? Although I took it along anyway.

Jerry Turnbull was 'old school' and we all took to him immediately. He was the archetypal Wing Commander. A small framed, grey haired man with a perfectly groomed RAF moustache and wearing a red flying suit with gold pilot wings embroidered on the left side of his chest. Very smart.

'Right,' said the Wingco. 'Get a weather forecast and present yourself back here in thirty minutes for a briefing and inflation.' Actually, the weather did not look good. The cloud was low and it was gusting. If we flew, we would have to get the balloon hot and quickly 'pop out' of the show ground to avoid the buildings. Downwind flag poles were also an obstacle as well as the grandstand, which was full of people. Nuneaton was also close to Coventry and Birmingham airports and entering airspace was a definite no go.

I rang Birmingham Airport for a forecast, telling them where I was planning the flight from and got the wind conditions at the surface, at 1,000, 2,000 and 5,000 feet. They informed me of speed and direction. The wind was gusting 10 to 15 knots on the ground, increasing to much higher speeds at altitude and in a direction heading straight into prohibited airspace. The final straw was that the cloud base was down to 400 feet making it impossible to fly without breaking the most rudimental rules of air law.

So I presented the facts to the Wingco in a clear concise manner which I thought would impress him in its clarity and the professional appreciation of the situation.

I said, 'Wingco, the met is 10 to 15 knots on the surface increasing to 15 to 20 knots at 1,000 feet, from 270 degrees that will take us directly into airspace. In addition to that there are immediate downwind obstacles in the showground and the cloud base is only 400 feet, so I conclude that the conditions are unsafe and not flyable.'

Jerry looked at me and said, 'Bollocks, we're flying! Brief the crew immediately.' Which I did, immediately.

Jerry was known to be very precise about briefing and listened to every word. I briefed them on the direction and speed of the winds. I reminded them not to enter the landing field unless they had permission from the farmer. I checked on their maps, money for a phone call to the retrieve number and went through the inflation process. I appointed a crown man and instructed the basket crew on how to weigh off and what words of instruction I would be giving. I emphasised that on no account, in any circumstances, were they to let their feet off the ground. That was an incredibly important instruction, particularly in gusty winds. The danger was a sudden gust that would lift a basket crew off the ground quickly. If they fell off at anything higher than 30 feet it would probably kill them. 'Never let your feet get off the ground' was an instruction that was constantly impressed upon the crew at every inflation. Jerry was nodding approval and we went into inflation mode. The balloon basket was secured by a tether rope to the chase vehicle and attached to the basket, with a karabiner, to be released at take off.

I was very nervous, but the inflation went off without a hitch, the crown line came in and I called for, 'Weight on the basket.' I invited Jerry to join me and he climbed in. I gave him the standard passenger brief, 'Hold on to the ropes in the basket. Do not touch the fuel cylinders or the burner unless I ask you to. I will tell you when we are landing. On landing bend your knees, ready for the impact, keep hold of the rope handles even after the balloon has stopped moving and do not leave the basket after landing until I tell you. I will repeat these instructions to you during the flight and immediately before we land. Understood?' I awaited a response.

'Perfectly,' he said and added, 'Do you mind if I ask you a question?' I nodded and he went on, 'Would it be helpful if I assisted the landing by deploying the trail rope for you – at your instruction, of course?'

He knew full well that I had forgotten all about that bloody trail rope. It was a nice thing to do, though, as it reminded me to attach one end of the trail rope to the burner frame. Chucking out an unattached 50 lbs ball of rope, in mid flight, would not have been a good thing.

The wind was blustery and gusting, and I needed to get away quickly and safely. A few burns to the balloon, set the altimeter, checked and record time, instructed 'hands off, hands on' and 'hands away' and off we lifted on my check out flight. We cleared the grandstand and I got the ascent absolutely right with the balloon snuggling under the cloud base at 400 feet. I checked the direction and speed. It was fast and we were heading straight into airspace, some forty-five minutes away. We had no ground to air, or air to air radio, so I could not contact the airport to warn them or ask permission to enter their airspace – they would have told me to bugger off anyway.

Like sailing ships on the water, balloons have right of way over powered vessels, but the air traffic controllers in the Coventry Airport control tower would not have been amused by having to send big jets around in circles while we gently drifted through their airspace. We had to land before we got into serious trouble, but there were only houses below us and we needed to clear the town first. Jerry was very experienced and not at all worried, waving to the householders below looking skyward from their gardens.

We cleared the edge of the town and we were moving quickly. I told Jerry that I was looking for a landing site and repeated the briefing for the landing. I looked at a grass field but there was a horse in it and in this wind speed, it was too small anyway. We were low at about 300 feet and the horse was running.

I vividly remember Jerry shouting, 'Canter' and the horse stopped immediately. No time to analyse that now, I could see the Coventry runway lights in the distance.

Jerry said to me, 'You may have to consider landing in crop.'

I retorted, 'I'm landing in the first big field that I can find, I don't care what it is.'

'Good decision,' he said, as I let the balloon descend to about 100 feet with my eye on a potential landing spot. It looked like a hayfield from where I was, which was a good option as hay is probably the cheapest crop and if you are about to destroy something, then that's about the least expensive option. As I descended further to a height of 50 feet and crossed the field boundary Jerry asked me if I wanted him to drop the trail rope yet.

I said, authoritatively, 'I will tell you when I'm ready,' then immediately shouted, 'Now!' I had forgotten all about that bloody trail rope, again! I then shouted, as I pulled on the rip line, 'Bend your knees and hold on to the rope handles. Do not get out of the balloon until I tell you. Even after it stops.'

The balloon touched down positively (that means hard in ballooning parlance) and as I pulled the parachute rip wide open, the basket went onto its side. We were in the customary drag situation as the wind took hold of the envelope and we sailed across the lovely, sweet smelling hay, carving out and flattening a basket wide section until we finally came to a stop.

We lay, side by side, in the basket for a few seconds and Jerry looked at me and said, quite calmly, 'That was very well done. Congratulations Captain! Can we get out now?'

We scrambled out of the basket and observed the 100 yards plus swathe of hay that we had flattened, just as the farmer entered the field. We walked towards him along the six feet wide path to the field perimeter and I contemplated what I was going to say to the farm owner. I had never landed in crop before but I knew the procedure as laid out by the British Balloon and Airship Club.

I extended my hand to the farmer and he said, 'Where have you come from? Is it cold up there? Looks bloody dangerous to me.'

I quickly explained, 'Look, I do apologise for landing in your hay, I am happy to measure out the damage and pay for it.'

Jerry added, 'We had a fuel tank problem, low pressure, so had no alternative.' That was the first I had heard of it, but I didn't give anything away.

The famer looked at the damaged crop and said, 'I wouldn't worry about that, would think about three quid would cover it. It might stand up again by tomorrow so don't be concerned. It does look bloody dangerous to me though,' he repeated.

The crew, having stopped to ask if anyone had seen a balloon, had been pointed in our direction. Observing a small crowd of people and parked cars at the entrance of the field, they pulled into the gate. I explained that our chase crew had arrived and the farmer gave his permission to enter the field. They pulled up along next to the start of the drag path and we packed the balloon away and carried the equipment out of the middle of the field, item by item and loaded it on to the trailer.

Next stop was the pub where we relived every second of the flight, burn by burn, the take off, the waving householders, the horse, the landing, the runway lights and the farmer. Everything. I asked Jerry about the horse stopping which had amazed me.

'Works every time,' Jerry told us. 'Shout *canter* and they just stop and stand there as if to say, "Where the fuck did that come from?" They are an animal of flight, they run from danger, but they don't have predators from the air and they don't think to look up. Horses are stupid!'

I don't think my wife will believe any of that, I thought. Anne was a keen rider and had her own horse and when I explained what had happened, she was extremely sceptical about all of it. I could not wait to test the theory again.

Jerry asked me for my log book and signed off the check out flight. He wrote, 'A good dual check out in blustery conditions. Fit to proceed to solo. Should practice the use of a trail rope in winds exceeding 10 knots.'

He gave me back the log book and advised me, with a nod, that I should notate that there was a problem with a fuel cylinder, giving poor fuel pressure, necessitating flying low and landing in crop, which I did. We said goodbye to the Wingco with much back slapping and hand shaking and a reminder from him that I owed him a duck supper.

So, finally it was done, although not quite. I needed to make a solo flight, observed and approved, from the ground, by an appointed captain. The thought of flying solo horrified me. Alone, in the basket, no one to advise me and no collective experience. I was not looking forward to it. Quite right too – in the end the flight nearly burned me to death.

Chapter Six

Going Solo

I still had a lot to do before becoming a fully functioning licensed pilot and spent the next month honing my skills. I was learning new landing techniques and collecting a series of instructor flights, with an appointed instructor. This would allow me to fly to conduct aerial advertising rather than socially with a Private Pilots Licence. Until I had completed those flights and my solo I would still be flying as a PUT.

I flew at the Royal showground in Stoneleigh and the Nottingham Royal Show from Trent Bridge. This type of show-flying was not easy. You took off from the main arena and had to get the balloon inflated and off the ground, in four minutes, without wiping out the grandstand and the people in it. It took precision timing and a great crew. We normally flew out of the arena as late as possible, to avoid thermal activity. A thermal is a pocket of hot air that can suddenly rise from the ground. On the ground, during inflation, thermals can be fierce and devastating, creating gusts from any direction, ripping the basket from the hands of the crew and throwing the balloon into the air before it crashes back down again. Not something you want to do in front of a packed grandstand.

During flight a big thermal can send a balloon to great altitudes and there is nothing you can do about it, you just have to go with it. A pilot must be able to recognise thermal activity; otherwise the balloon can rise even though the hot air is cooling inside the envelope. Unless you keep it warm, which is not instinctive while the balloon is rising in a thermal, it will come out of the thermal cold and scream down to the ground. Thermals are probably one of the most frightening natural phenomena for the balloon pilot. There are a few others.

So we would take off from an arena to make a very short duration flight, normally landing in the showground car park. After all, these were commercial flights and there was little point in flying over the countryside exposing the logo to a million cows. So the car parks were also the preferred balloon landing site, but you had to come in steep and quick as thousands of parked cars were a hazard. Left standing in the sunlight for several hours the car bodywork could become very hot indeed, creating its own microclimate. The generated heat would create the sudden release of thermals which were sharp enough to distort balloon envelopes and low level wind shear as the pockets of hot air rose rapidly to altitude. I have seen several balloons bouncing off the roofs of parked cars.

With the advent of parachute rips we were writing new landing techniques. I found that on approach to landing you could crack open the parachute, letting limited air out and controlling the descent perfectly. With the new very powerful burners pushing out up to 12 million BTU (Thursday's Child was one million) in unison with the parachute rip, you could adjust your rise and fall rate very accurately. We all began to 'profile fly', sailing across fields at low level, up and over trees, brushing the uppermost leaves and back down to a foot above the surface, crossing lakes and rivers with the basket dribbling along the surface of the water. There was no better flight experience. It was, well, idyllic.

Now rotation vents had been introduced to balloon envelopes. Two slits, on each side of the balloon with operating lines running to the basket. Pull the left vent open and the escaping air would slowly spin to the balloon left, the opposite way if you pulled the right line. I think it was developed to allow the pilot to turn the basket in the direction he was facing for landing, without moving the passengers in a sometimes packed basket.

However, I saw another use. It meant that you could turn the balloon logo to face the camera. There was nothing more annoying for the client than seeing a newspaper photograph or TV footage of the balloon showing half of their logo. All of our pilots were to become well trained in that procedure. The trick was to identify where the cameras were – in the grandstand, on the launch site, in other balloons and make sure you flew past them with the logo fully displayed. There is a surprising amount of steerage available on a balloon flight, with ribbons of air in different directions at different altitudes. Generally, summer flying, when most of the agricultural shows were scheduled, flights were conducted in high pressure systems (anti cyclones). In these conditions the rotating motion of our planet means that a balloon would turn right as it ascended and, conversely, left as we descended from altitude. This applies to the northern hemisphere. Below the equator the opposite rules apply. In general the wind would also increase with altitude, so using this basic knowledge we would bounce off the various winds to steer the balloons into suitable camera positions.

Meanwhile, running up to my solo flight, I also did three local flights from Quatt, near my home in Bridgnorth, and had the opportunity to test out the horse theory, several times. It actually worked, but you had to shout the command in the correct way with a cadence that the horse would recognise. My wife Anne, who keeps her own horses and is an enthusiastic dressage rider, explained how to enunciate the commands properly. Normally the command 'canter' is instructed with the emphasis on both syllables can-ter. Trot is normally ter-rot and walk is waaalk. I tried all of these commands but for some reason can-ter was the most effective. I tried it several times and reported back to my wife but she was still not convinced. I would have to demonstrate this to her soon. As soon as I had completed my solo flight and obtained my licence.

It is important to appreciate hot air balloon flight conditions to understand how well sounds travel from the basket. In flight the balloon is moving at the speed of the wind, so, effectively, you are in still air and apart from the intermittent use of the burners, which emit a huge roar and explains why I am now deaf, it would be silent in the basket, save for the quiet hissing of a pilot light which ignites the burners. You can communicate with people on the ground quite effectively. I have often spoken to people as I have flown over their garden from 500 feet. They are normally staring intently up at you and I would always speak to them. 'Good morning.' They could hear it clearly but often do not understand where it is coming from and look around, from side to side as if to say 'Who's saying that?' So I would wave and say, 'It's me. In the balloon.'

'HI,' they would shout. 'WHERE ARE YOU GOING?'

I would point in the direction we were flying and say, 'That way, and you don't have to shout.' I would often have conversations with them, including asking directions to the nearest pub, talking about the lovely weather etc.

They always had smiles on their face. Balloons do make people smile and dogs bark. So it was undeniable that horses could hear us speaking to them. They just did not know where the voice was coming from. It is also undeniable that balloons, with burners at full blast, make a terrible din, so any responsible pilot would keep a sharp look out for any type of livestock. Horses, in particular, could be very expensive animals and had a propensity when scared out of their wits to run into objects or simply have a fatal heart attack. All stock, including cattle, sheep and pigs, were to be given a wide berth. There was a general rule of not landing in occupied grass fields if at all possible. If in difficulty, crop was the next option and a field with a full stock was to be avoided at all costs. So during my local training flights I was always aware of not messing up in my own backyard and went to considerable lengths to generate a good relationship with the local farming community.

We took off one morning just after dawn, in Thursday's Child, in an effort to rack up the hours before my solo flight. The inflation and take off were uneventful, the speed aloft was a steady 10 knots at 1,000 feet and we flew for an hour under a cloudy sky, practising landing approaches, straight and level flight and generally having a good time. I saw a large field ahead that was clear of stock and no sign of a stray horse or anything on the approach. There was a track going from the field, through some out- buildings, past the farmhouse to the road which offered easy access for the chase crew, which would be able to call at the house on their way to the field to obtain permission from the farmer. Perfect.

'That's the one,' I said and pointed to the spot, briefing the passengers on the landing procedure. It was a faultless approach, low over the outbuildings and into the field with a 4 knot surface wind. A pull on the rip line and over the balloon went, a short drag of 15 yards to a stop. Super. We made the deflated balloon safe, walked down the aforementioned track and went to look for the chase crew, past a very large and modern barn. As we went around the corner of the barn to the front end there was a woman standing there leaning with her back against a door, smoking a cigarette. I can only describe her as, well, looking ill. She had short hair and wore a lightweight brown jacket, fawn skirt and wellington boots, all of which were splattered with white blobs. I thought she must have been painting the barn.

Our 'good mornings' elicited no response, not even a movement of her head so I said, 'Excuse me, madam, are you all right?'

'No,' she said, 'I am certainly not all right. I have twenty thousand turkeys in there. There was this sudden, frightful roaring sound. Every one of them took off and every one of them shat on me! I thought a plane must have crashed!'

So on August 2 1977 I took Thursday's Child to Patshull Park to make my first solo flight, observed from the ground by Tony Gough. Thursday's Child was looking a little tired now. The fabric was getting porous, although it had passed its annual Certificate of Airworthiness which always included a grab test on the fabric to make sure it had not weakened. It was also looking a little dated. A single burner, not multi-gimballed, steel fuel tanks, rather than the new aluminium lightweight types and, worst of all, a banana rip. She was an old lady, with only a tenth of the burn power of Woolworths and she needed to be treated with respect.

The Met forecast was reasonable, the wind coming from the east which, with a bit of luck, would take me in the direction of Bridgnorth.

A westerly wind was a no go as it went straight into Wolverhampton and since there are no landing areas until the other side of Birmingham and into airspace, it was not even an option. Anyway, the old lady did not have the duration to make such a flight. By that time in my flying career our inflation protocol had progressed a little and we always carried a small bottle of helium and some small latex balloons on the chase vehicle. The crew released one from the launch field to confirm the wind speed and direction.

'Yes, it's 5 to 8 knots, easterly to Bridgnorth,' I said, studying the map carefully. I then drew two lines on the map to indicate wind direction on the surface and at 2,000 feet wind which provided me with a sector in which I would, or should, be flying. I knew the area well, had planned for a flight of no more than thirty minutes, predicted the approximate landing area, inflated the balloon and took off. I ascended to 800 feet with the infamous lake below me and took a compass bearing of the launch site to verify the direction. Straight towards Wolverhampton! I hated solo flights already even though this was the first one I had done. I looked over each side of the basket to double check. No doubt about it, I was going the wrong way.

'Bugger,' I shouted to no one but myself. 'Hey,' I thought 'Don't panic.' I had made a few difficult flights before. I was bound to find a field, even if it was crop, in the short distance I had before hitting the outskirts of the town. 'It will be fine,' I said to myself. 'Just fine.'

Then all hell let loose.

The brass valve on the metal cylinder ruptured for no apparent reason and a jet of volatile, highly inflammable liquid propane gas spewed, under pressure, into the basket hitting me at crutch level. Propane is freezing cold, boils at -42 °C and burns you instantly. I quickly reached for the thick asbestos gloves that were standard equipment in all baskets and attempted to turn off the valve. I managed to staunch it a lot, but a constant spray of gas was still shooting out, albeit at a lower pressure. My trousers had frozen solid on the right side and were crumbling and falling off. That was the least of my problems. My right hand had cold burns and the balloon was starting to descend, which meant the pilot light was going to catch up with the gas cloud leak any second. That would be it. I had no alternative. I switched off the pilot light and now had no means of getting any heat into the balloon. I did have another cylinder coming from the opposite side of the basket but there was no way I could light it with the cloud of gas in the basket. I had two choices, to risk a fire and certain death or to take my chances when hitting the ground. I chose the latter.

The balloon was coming down and I was now two fields away from the first house on the edge of the town. As I stood there contemplating my fate, my right trouser leg fell around my ankle. I was about to fly over an oak tree and I made an instant and instinctive decision. I pulled the rip and took the top out of the balloon. The basket crashed into the tree, which was hard and unforgiving British oak. And then I got lucky. The weight of the hot air that remained in the envelope pulled me through the tree and I landed, softly, in the field. The crash had somehow stopped the leak and I crawled out the basket and got very religious.

I stood by the side of the basket, with one trouser leg and a broken little finger on my left hand and I thought 'Well, a broken finger, cold burns and I look a right tit but it's better than being dead!' I stepped away from the basket and reached for a cigarette, lit it and took a big draw. At that precise moment the valve went again and a huge cloud of gas poured from the basket. I ran like hell, towards the crew, who had just entered the field. I blurted out the story, adding, 'Don't go near the basket, it could go off like a bomb! I've bust my finger and burnt my trousers, hand and bollocks!'

We waited until the balloon was safe to handle and eventually retired to the Mermaid public house with sticky tape (balloon repair tape) holding up the right leg of my trousers. The burns were not too bad, just skin deep, but the finger hurt. We had a few pints and a good laugh.

There was a young couple on the chase crew, Andria and her partner Bev Dale. They were my main balloon crew and gave me wonderful, tireless and uncomplaining support over many memorable years.

Andria said, 'We came into the field and saw you running, holding one hand in the air, a fag in the other, with your trousers round your ankles and I thought, "Christ, he's gone mad."'

I kept that faulty cylinder, as a reminder, and still have it to this day.

Throughout these early years of ballooning I learned a technique of how to relax before the moment of impact. Ballooning, at that time, was all about hitting the ground or a tree or building, unscheduled and very hard. There were many injuries occurring on a daily basis to balloon pilots. We were all learning as we flew along and I was advised by an ex-racing driver that a relaxed body is less likely to break than a body held taught and stiff – with the anticipation of impending injury. So while I always held on tightly to avoid being ejected from the basket, I trained myself to let my body go limp in the split second before impact. The close your eyes, grit your teeth and hang on for grim death was definitely not to be used to minimise the possibility of serious damage and injury.

Chapter Seven

Back to Balloons and Racing Tyres

While I was travelling the world and flying balloons, my brother Jonathan had researched a competition tyre manufactured, in Japan, by Yokohama Tyres. The tyre had a good reputation in Japan but was not sold in Europe. We sent them a telex asking to see them and they agreed. I funded a trip to Tokyo for Jonathan and myself to visit them. It was a rather cheeky move since we had little money to do this and Tokyo was an expensive destination. We flew the polar route to Japan, economy class, via Anchorage, Alaska, arriving at Narita Airport with little money but a lot of 'front'.

We checked into a small hotel called the Dai-ichi in the fashionable Shimbashi area and during the next few years this became our favoured place to stay in Tokyo. The hotel had a spa which we visited frequently. It featured a large Jacuzzi and the procedure was to spend some time in that and then immediately jump into a cold bath in water up to our necks. Following that you would proceed to the traditional Japanese washing room where you would sit around a communal circular bath, naked, to wash yourself. Once dry, we would dress in shorts and a light gown, issued by the hotel, before proceeding into the massage room where the most skilful of young, bare footed ladies, dressed only in shorts and T-shirt, would give you the world's best total body massage. It would include walking along your back, clicking in any vertebrae that were out of place. Finally, you would go to the rest area, wrapped in a cosy, thick dressing gown, to rest in a reclining chair for twenty minutes while, for some unexplained but obvious health reason, they served you hard boiled eggs and lime juice. It was a wonderful experience and always set us up for the long and protracted meetings with the Yokohama management team.

Somehow we managed to convince them that we were the people to distribute the products in Europe. The Yokohama management team conducted themselves in the typical Japanese manner and the company was very good. I could eat anything they placed before me, except on one occasion. Freshness was the key word in Tokyo and the sushi bars and restaurants were the 'in places'. The fresher the better was the main objective and one night Sekicowa San, a Yokohama Tyres marketing executive, took us to an eating establishment that he told us had the finest reputation for freshness in Tokyo. Unfortunately, it was also enormously expensive and we were always nervous that we would run out of cash. The damage caused by being unable to pay for a meal would have been incalculable. Loss of face is very important to the Japanese and somehow we had to convince them that we could raise large sums of money to pay for containers of tyres.

During our trips to Japan, we tried to immerse ourselves into the culture of the country as much as possible, soaking up the atmosphere of the cherry blossom covered trees in the streets of Tokyo during May and eating in local restaurants. We also played Pachinko in the local arcades, trying to understand the Japanese fascination in such a mind-numbingly boring game, taking the bullet train to the historical town of Kyoto, with its winding streets, alleys and craft shops that have been handed down to families for generations, with traditionally dressed girls with pixie feet, trip trapping daintily to perform the famous tea ceremonies. Returning to Tokyo and passing the majestic Mount Fuji, the iconic snow capped, still active volcano standing alone in a blue oriental sky overlooking a landscape of paddy fields.

So I was well up for this evening and Sekicowa San ordered the prawns for all of us. They were taken out of the tanks and peeled, the head left on, and placed on a plate still alive. Sekicowa San demonstrated how to eat them. Picking up a giant prawn with his chop sticks he dipped the tail of the invertebrate into the wasabi mustard on his plate, explaining that this relish made them tingle and move around a bit. He then bit off the peeled body and swallowed it. Following that he deftly opened the shell, behind the head and out dropped the stomach sack, a greenish, glutinous mass dangling by a thread attached to the back of the head. It was then swallowed whole and considered a great delicacy. But not by me. I did try and raised the body to my mouth, with the chopsticks, after dipping the tail into the wasabi. I moved the tail to my lips but as it touched my tongue it was still wriggling and all of its antennae on the head were waving gently in front of me, its eyes trying to look at what was going on behind. I simply could not eat it, which, fortunately, our Japanese guest thought was highly amusing.

We arrived back to the UK having secured the Japanese contract. It was a business that needed a lot of money. Containers of high performance racing and competition tyres were going to mean raising a lot of cash which we had to borrow from banks and financial institutions. It was an enormous risk and I had to offer up personal guarantees, using my home as collateral. Jonathan was young and obviously did not have the assets available to support such borrowings.

We had now secured two new balloon contracts for Bluebird Toffees and the Staffordshire Building Society and Lighter Than Air Ltd, with a stable of four balloons, was generating some revenue. We were hiring pilots for weekend events, attending shows in all parts of the country, entertaining crowds of people who seemed fascinated at the spectacle of this exciting form of flight.

As time passed the racing tyre business was also growing as we appointed distributers across the country and began to establish Yokohama racing products as a credible brand of tyres.

Before we commissioned the Bluebird Toffee and Staffordshire Building Society balloons I learned of a new hot air balloon manufacturer in Ireland, owned by a chap called Per Lindstrand and I was impressed with his approach to the market. Instead of buying a balloon with the optional extras of double burners, parachute rips, rotation vents and Flexi ridged poles to hold the burner aloft from the basket, Per only sold balloons fully kitted with all this equipment. I ordered the new balloons from his factory and negotiated a distributorship of Lindstrand Balloons for the UK market. They were high quality, well made aerostats with new type stainless steel Worcester fuel valves and padded leather tops to the baskets, all fitted as standard. I took a two page spread in the British Balloon and Airship Club magazine, The Aerostat, to advertise this innovative new approach to ballooning. It was a relationship with Per that was to last for more than thirty years.

I was still quite an inexperienced pilot and would fly any time I could to get the hours into my log book, winter and summer. In fact, one of the most memorable and pleasant flights of my entire flying career took place on a cold winter's day. It was a surreal experience. I was flying the Woolworths balloon with Tony Gough in a stiff breeze, at 1,500 feet, when it started to snow. Snow and rain are not pleasant during a balloon flight. The rain makes the envelope heavy and can force the balloon down. You would think that you were underneath the world's biggest brolly and that's true to a point but the rain water can cascade down the envelope and pour into the baskets in torrents. It is to be avoided at all costs; it can make controlled flying difficult and get the envelope very wet and heavy. Once wet it has to be dried before storing, as moisture in the tightly packed balloon in its bag can send the fabric mouldy. However, this was snow, now falling heavily in large flakes. I descended to look for a landing site when the most peculiar of things happened. The balloon descent rate began to increase and matched the fall rate of the snow. It seemed the world had stopped and it scrambled our senses. The balloon was surrounded by millions of snowflakes which were suspended, dead still around us. It was weird and fascinating and as we descended faster the snowflakes starting going upwards, or appeared so. This was an experience and sensation that the brain was unable to configure and I realised it was utterly impossible to achieve in any other

How it all began. Thursday's Child with the Dudley Zoo name stitched onto the envelope, in an early attempt to circumvent the aerial advertising rules

Left: *Water trial of the capsule at Stoney Cove in the UK. Dave Omerod and the diving team rehearsing the rescue procedures.* **Right:** *The team of divers at Stoney Cove, practicing the rescue for a future North Sea landing*

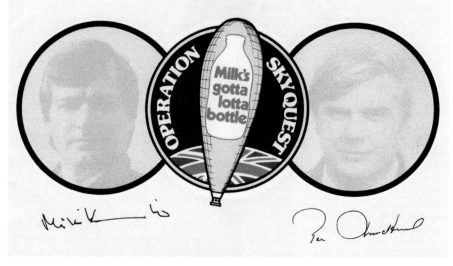

The promotional brochure, produced for the project

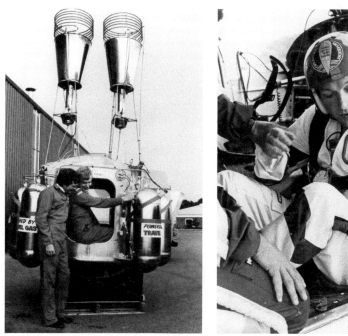

Left: *The capsule is shipped to the USA to make the altitude attempt*
Right: *Into a small Cessna aircraft for my first parachute jump*

Left: One of the many test flights for the Operation Sky Quest altitude attempt, which all went horribly wrong. ***Right:*** *The Operation Sky Quest capsule on exhibition at Weston Park in the UK. I am holding my young son Robert*

The first inflation attempt for Operation Sky Quest in Watton UK. Note Per Lindstrand hanging on to the balloon at the crown (left). He broke the first rule of ballooning for ground crews – never let your feet off the ground. He fell and injured himself, just before the balloon's fabric split and we decided to move the project to the USA

Left: The Lindstrand balloon built for a promotion of BRMB Radio
Right: Ozzy Osbourne is aboard this flight, which started at a pub and ended in a pub

Left: The ice cream cone built for the Royal Show in Stoneleigh, from where it made its maiden flight. The registration as G-ICES. Right: A small, one man replica of the altitude attempt balloon. It zipped across the sky and frightened the life out of me

Left: The first real contract for my company Lighter Than Air Ltd
Right: The record attempt is over. The balloon rips from its moorings just as we were about to get into the capsule

Left: One of my pilot training flights in Thursday's Child. I generated the animal shapes from a Rupert the Bear annual. ***Right:*** The Bluebird balloon was the second contract for Lighter Than Air Ltd and was our first balloon built by Per Lindstrand

The first flight in the Sudan. In the north it was a nice and sandy desert, great for take off and landings

Left: This rather unpleasant smelling tribe did not want us to leave their village, until we had treated all of the sick warriors. Right: As we moved south, in Sudan, the balloon began to show signs of damage. This picture was taken by Leo Dickinson who was hanging onto a rope ladder to get pictures from unusual angles

In the Sudan, every Monday was Banks's night, wherever we were. This time in a village named Dinder on the Ethiopian boarder

Anne on board a camel at the Omdurman camel sales in Sudan. She is frantically trying to get the camel driver to keep his hands to himself

A rather fuzzy picture taken from a long distance. It shows David Howerski clinging onto the rope ladder below the balloon. He had jumped from the basket and landed back on the balloon. The first time anyone had jumped out of an aircraft and landed back on it

Left: A preflight inspection before my son Robert's first flight. Note registration G-Roby. *Right: Robert's first flight in a balloon named after him. Note the bottle of gripe water in my hand*

The delivery of Woolworths balloon. From left to right. Dick Hamp, myself, Steve Laugharne, Rob Jones, Pilot Tony Gough and Dick Wirth

Left: The Milk Marketing Board cloudhopper balloon during a live broadcast for the Michael Aspel TV show. My right leg still in plaster after a parachuting incident in Florida. *Right:* My first jump from 14,000 feet is completed. Mitch Decoteau is telling me how well I had done!

The doctor holding the x-ray pictures. Left to right, me on crutches with Tom Donnelly, the doctor and nurse

Myself and Per all ready to step into the capsule for a test flight at 40,000 feet

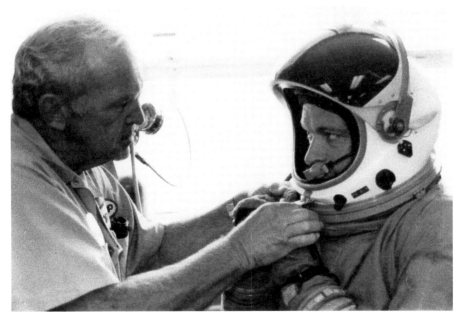

A NASA technician fits me into an Apollo spacesuit.
It was an option but too expensive

Above: Per and I arriving at the Johnson Space Centre in Houston, Texas, as we move the project to the USA

Left: Getting togged up for a flight in the capsule. Parachute, pressure suit and oxygen mask

Facing the press immediately after the balloon had escaped. The attempt was off and out of money

The Staffordshire Building Society also realised the branding value of hot air balloons. Note my two eldest sons have their fingers in their ears. Burners were very noisy, which is why I am now deaf!

My first demonstration to a potential client. My fashionable long hair and whiskers were instantly removed a few minutes later

It's showtime at the Dudley Hippodrome. Me sandwiched between the then current world heavyweight champion, Mike Marino and the contender Wayne Bridges. Photograph by Don Smith

Left: My first trip to Egypt to ascertain if tourist ballooning would be possible. I felt unable to control the camel so switched to a horse... I couldn't control that either

Below: I took the Royal Mail balloon to Germany in 1988. Princess Anne came to see the balloon and I almost got her into the basket for a flight

We only had a day to practice the skydive before we jumped out of the aircraft. Most of it was taken up by hanging from a tree, practising body position and pulling the rip cord. Left to right Rowland Hilfiker, Tom Donnelly and Mitch Decoteau

Some flights were just for fun. Me and my wife Anne with Per Lindstrand. Note the double burners, now standard on all balloons and the upright posts holding the burner above the basket

way. The balloon had suspended animation and seemed to have frozen nature in a moment of complete silence and stillness. It was wonderfully strange.

I was clocking up the hours, particularly with Thursday's Child, promoting the zoo in the immediate catchment area around the 'Black Country', so named due to the soot and pollution caused by iron and steel production in the 19th century. This area is rich in its own mini-culture and is a favourite part of the country for me. You have to understand the Black Country to enjoy it. It has its own strong dialect that is difficult for people outside of the area to understand. It is impossible for overseas visitors to comprehend. And I love it.

The problem is that some of the vowels in the dialect are transposed. The E becomes an A so 'that' becomes 'thet', while 'peas' becomes 'pays' but not all of the time. Some local words and phrases are completely substituted when 'isn't it?' becomes 'aye it?' and the word 'aye' can also mean 'have not' as well as 'is not' and when this is delivered with a broad accent it can be confusing with the added complication of a sort of cockney rhyming slang. Pub names are often changed. I have never heard the Five Ways pub referred to by that name. It is always referred to by the locals as 'The Widow's', as it was kept by a widow a hundred years ago. The Vine is called 'The Bull and Bladder', as it was built on the site of a slaughterhouse.

So when strangers stop a local to ask for directions, which in the UK, normally uses pubs as navigation points, the enquirer is left completely bewildered as they search for invisible pub names.

One night in The Bull and Bladder I asked a local chap called Graham why he did not bring his wife to the pub and he replied 'Well, yow car pureron page thray, but hers good to liwith, thet's the kay aye it?' Meaning, 'you can't put her on page three (The Sun, a UK tabloid newspaper), but she is good to live with, that is the key, is it not?' This enclave and the characters in it are still alive and well in this part of the Black Country. It is unique and I savour my time and visits there.

I was still running TV news pieces for Central News and produced a story concerning a local chap simply known as Caggy. It came from caggy (left) handed. He was a bargeman and ran a barge up and down the canal (cut) pulled by his horse (hoss), hauling coal or any other cargo he could find. The local reporter was John Swallow who conducted the interview with Caggy standing by his horse and the barge.

He asked Caggy how long he had been doing this and he replied, 'I've bin walkin' this cut for nigh on fifty 'ear and wi this hoss for 20 'ear.'

'I see,' said John. 'And what makes a good, er horse?'

'What meks a good hoss?' Caggy asked rhetorically. 'I'll tell yow what meks a good hoss, look 'ere.' He then put his hand on the horse's flank and moved it down its withers and as the camera followed his hand, John bent down to see. Caggy then pointed at his horse's penis and said, 'Yow ever sin a weapon on an hoss like thet?'

John, still in a bent over position, turned his head to the camera and quietly said, 'Cut.'

It was a funny moment and we retired to the Bull and Bladder for a pint of the very strong Bathams locally brewed ale. One of the locals was a chap known as Sam the Pig and he always went into the pub at the same time every night to have three pints on the trot. As he was drinking the first, the landlady was pulling the second which he immediately consumed while the empty glass was refilled again. The only way to describe the way he drank each pint is that, without pausing for breath, he chucked down the beer with a chewing motion and hence earned the name they gave him. I don't know how he stood up after three pints. I could never manage more than one and a half over a couple of hours. It was, and still is, a wonderful pub that had not changed for years. It was decorated in a sort of fifties style with neon strip lights in the lounge. I took my PA and an admin girl there one night and they were mesmerised by the treatment they were subjected to. One ordered a gin and tonic which was sort of OK but the other asked for a dry Martini and tonic, which clearly had the barman flustered.

'A dry what?' he enquired.

'Martini,' Sarah replied sweetly.

The landlord turned his head towards an open trap door which led to the cellar and shouted, 'Ruth, we got anything called Martini?' The voice from the cellar told him that there was some on the shelf in a green bottle, which he located, then dusted off the bottle and poured a generous measure into a half pint glass!

'Could we have some ice, please?' asked the girls.

After a short stare at the girls the landlord tilted his head to shout down the cellar steps. 'Ruth, these posh tarts want to know if we got any ice.'

'We doe do ice,' came the reply. 'Tell 'em to piss off.'

Still on the theme of this wonderful and unusual dialect, one day we had finished a windy tether display at a school in Gornal Wood and went back to the house in Gornal of one of the parents. Over tea (tae) he informed his wife that Ray the Bag was coming to see them. I didn't know the origin of the name Ray the Bag, but 'bag' is a word often used in the Black Country idiom. Uncomplimentary phrases were common like, 'Her's a good wench but her's got a face like a bag a spanners', meaning she was ugly. Or 'Her's got a face like a bag of pork scratchings', meaning her complexion was something other than flawless.

It was explained to me that Ray the Bag's missus was pregnant and that she was 'about to drap it' (drop it). That they already had two saucepans (saucepan lids - kids) but they were both girls and they were hoping for one 'with a spout'. Ray came into the house and they excitedly enquired if she had indeed, drapped it, which was immediately confirmed.

'Is it a bloke?' asked my host.

'Nah,' Ray the Bag replied in a rather resigned manner. 'It's another double arsed un,' and we went to the Widow's pub to 'wet the saucepan's 'ead.

The pub had a local talent night in full swing with an organ player accompanying singers who all seemed to perform in their own peculiar style. There was a rendition of 'If I Ruled the World', sung as… 'If I ruled the world, ah. Every day would be the first day of spring, ah, every heart would have a new song to sing, ahh' while we drank the local ale and ate cheese and black pudding cobs. It was a place full of real people, drinking real ale and having a real good time.

After the Bluebird and Staffordshire balloons were delivered to our storage facility, Per Lindstrand moved the factory to Oswestry, just 30 miles away from my office. He had lots of new ideas and he became a great friend. He had some wonderful plans and was what I would later refer to as a concept engineer. The concepts and innovations often sounded amazing but did not always work as expected, as I was to find out to my cost.

Meanwhile, Africa was calling again. Richard Barr and another pilot friend of his, Ian McDonald, had come up with an idea to fly across the Sudan and we met to discuss the feasibility of such a madcap idea. The plan was to take a balloon expedition, beginning from the town of Wadi Halfa, located at the northern Sudan border with Egypt, and then follow the route of the Nile to the southern tip of the country. The Sudan was a little known country, the largest in Africa, and this was an exciting prospect. It needed money and I set about securing it, eventually succeeding in getting Harlech Television to fund the expedition and make a TV documentary of the trip. The producer, Aled Vaughn, was intrigued by the idea and we settled on a fee of £12,000 that would cover the cost. We did not have a 'hook' for the story, a reason for doing it, and when Aled asked me all I could come up with was that we were doing this 'for the hell of it'.

He accepted that and used the phrase in marketing the programme to the TV networks. It was essential to sell the documentary to the networks so that Harlech TV could recover its costs. The working title for the project, which would later change, was 'Balloon Over Sudan', it was a complex and difficult undertaking and we needed to build a team that had varying skill sets. That team comprised of myself (expedition leader and pilot), Richard Barr and Ian MacDonald, who had brought the idea to me, Dick Hamp (pilot) Giles Hall (pilot and general good egg), Rob Jones (expedition engineer), Liz Seawood (pilot and medic) and army Captain Chris Beal (logistics).

It was an enormous undertaking. Although we built two balloons for the expedition, the second balloon was really only used to film the lead aerostat and of course would be a back-up if we had a disaster with the first balloon.

A major responsibility was the spares and repairs package that needed to be assembled. This would include a sewing machine to stitch up the inevitable rips to the envelope and a generator to power the sewing machine. Bob Jones, the now appointed expedition engineer, was just the sort of chap that could fix anything the Sudan could throw at us. We also needed to take an inflatable boat with an outboard motor to rescue the balloon and crew in the event of a river ditching. Chris looked after the feeding requirements and obtained army rations for all of the crew for a one month-long trip and ground to air radios to communicate with the flyers.

Personal arms were required and I obtained a firearms certificate for a Browning 9mm semi-automatic pistol while others preferred to take shotguns. Liz, who was actually a dentist, put together medical supplies including anti-venom injections for snake bites, plus medication and treatments for the more predicable ailments of cuts and bruises, diarrhoea, sunstroke, salt deprivation and general sickness.

The final member of the team was David Howerski, an ex-special services soldier who knew how to live and survive in dangerous territories, and who would instruct us on how to parachute out of the basket in the event of an emergency. Monday nights was always our night at the pub and I decided to keep this tradition flowing and take along a fridge and a large supply of Banks's bitter. I knew it was going to be a long and hard trip and I thought we should have a social evening every Monday, no matter where we were, to vent our frustration and share stories over a pint of cold English beer. It is these kind of small things that are simple to add but can make a big difference in difficult situations. I contacted Banks's Brewery and spoke to its publicity manager Peter Murdoch. I told him we wanted Banks's Beer to be the official beer of our expedition. He was intrigued and I agreed to meet him at Patshull Park with

Thursday's Child in tow. We inflated the balloon in readiness for his arrival, attaching it to the chase vehicle on a 100 feet tether line. Driving up to a fully inflated balloon impresses most people and we received the anticipated comments, with Peter telling us how magnificent it looked. I had difficulty getting him into the basket though, he seemed very nervous. I took the balloon up to the end of the tether a couple of times before he reluctantly agreed to get in. I learned that Patshull Park was, in fact, a place where Peter had spent a few months in its rehabilitation centre, convalescing after a fall off a mountain side, having had an attack of vertigo. No wonder he was reluctant to get into the balloon. He hung on to the baskets rope handles very tightly during the tethered flight and got very sweaty indeed.

He did agree to supply Balloon Over Sudan with the beer though, and agreed to meet after we got back from Africa as I told him I wanted to build a balloon in the shape of a pint glass of Banks's beer, with a basket shaped in the form of a beer barrel.

Harlech TV had appointed Leo Dickinson as the cameraman, a well-known adventure filmmaker with a well deserved reputation of producing unusual film sequences in extreme situations and we sat in my office discussing new ways of shooting the footage. The name of the game in adventure filmmaking, Leo explained, was to get shots from angles that the viewer had not seen before. Leo was also an experienced skydiver and was prepared to place himself and his camera in risky situations, fastened to the balloon hanging from ropes from anywhere from which he could parachute away from if anything went wrong. We discussed attaching a rope ladder from the crown of the balloon to the basket from which Leo could strap himself on to, giving a unique camera angle across the basket from his position 40 feet away.

As we were talking we came up with a plan for David Howerski, who was also a very experienced parachutist and skydiver. We could mount cameras on their helmets which would provide very exciting shots jumping out of the balloon baskets. Then came the coup de grâce.

What if we suspended the rope ladder beneath the baskets with

David in the basket and Leo on the rope ladder? The balloon would climb to over 10,000 feet; David would jump out getting a snatch shot of Leo on the rope ladder hanging below the basket. The balloon could then quickly descend to the same level as the parachute, while David filmed the balloon as he flew around it and could eventually fly on to the rope ladder and climb back into the basket! It would be the first time that anyone had jumped from an aircraft and landed back on it, intentionally anyway. Was it possible? Yes. Was it dangerous? Yes. Would it make good footage? Again, yes. That was three good reasons why we should have a crack at it. As it turned out all those three elements proved to be the case.

This Sudan trip was to feature later, illustrated pictorially, in Leo Dickinson's book 'Filming the Impossible' which included photographic images of the expedition, including all of the parachute jumps and all of the balloons flights, capturing David's attempt to be the first person to jump out of – and land back into - a hot air balloon. David also recommended that I should learn how to make a parachute jump, due to the nature of flying we were envisaging in the Sudan. Hot air balloons had not been flown in quite this way before and the stresses and loadings we were to impart on the envelopes were unknown. He advised that it may be prudent to know how to get out of the basket, to safety, if anything terrible happened. The thought of making a parachute jump appalled me, but I knew it made sense and I went to his parachute training centre with my heart in a sling as I prepared to jump out of a perfectly serviceable aircraft. This was not a 'tandem jump' for a charity, as is often undertaken nowadays, this was a static line jump from low altitude (2,000 feet), purely to learn how to save myself in the event of some catastrophic failure of the balloon.

I spent an entire day at ground school learning PLFs (Parachute Landing Falls), feet together, knees bent and the routine of practising the deploying of the reserve parachute, in the event of the main chute not opening. The exit from the aircraft was simulated, learned and rehearsed on the ground, in monotonous repetition until it was firmly imprinted in the brain. Arms folded across the chest, shouting, 'One thousand, two thousand, three thousand CHECK.' On the CHECK word, if the main shoot had not deployed, left hand to the reserve handle, right hand on top of it, 'PULL.'

The parachute I was using was a standard 20 foot navy conical, no steering toggles, it just brought you straight down. I did this jump from a small aircraft and could not understand why anyone would ever do this for fun. David asked if I would like to learn how to pack the parachutes, but I politely declined. I had no intention of ever undertaking this exercise again except in a dire emergency. That turned out to be another inaccurate forecast.

Chris Beal was dispatched to Khartoum to set things up and returned to the UK to inform us that upon his arrival he met with the British Military attaché, Dicky Bird, and had recruited a section of Sudanese soldiers to accompany us on our journey across the Sudan. They would be fully armed with the traditional Kalashnikovs and led by a Sudanese Intelligence Officer, a certain Major Marhdi. The Sudan Army had also agreed to supply two Land Rovers and two six wheel drive Magirus Deutz wagons to transport the crew and equipment.

So it was in January 1979, I found myself on a Sudan Air flight from London's Heathrow bound for Khartoum. It held a container full of balloons, food rations, generator, sewing machines, some weaponry, medical kit, Banks's beer and a fridge!

We were a group of very excited, if somewhat apprehensive balloonatics, ready to start a new African adventure that would create memories to last a lifetime.

In those days personal guns and ammunition were taken, by a policeman, to the cockpit for safe keeping until arrival at the destination when the captain would hand them over to the authorities before they released them to us. The captain was a senior British Airways pilot, Keith Fairy, on secondment to Sudan Air. During the flight he invited us into the cockpit and we talked about his love for the Sudan and its people. He asked us if he could join us for the first leg of the journey and

I readily agreed. We had enough provisions for an extra person and his experience might prove invaluable. We shook hands on the arrangement as the Sudan Air Boeing 727 lowered its landing gear for the approach into Khartoum International airport.

Chapter Eight

Balloon Over Sudan

We arrived in Khartoum to a bright blue African sky and a plague of locusts. There were literally millions of them, large two inch long flying insects that were infesting this great African capital city. You crunched them as they lay on the floor where you walked and they smothered every available surface, landing on us as we moved through Khartoum immigration. They infested our clothes and got in our hair. I found this very uncomfortable; I don't like creepy crawlies anyway and jumped every time I was targeted by these beastly creatures.

The plan was to stay at the Sudan Hotel on the esplanade in front of the Nile for a couple of days until we headed off into the desert and began the journey south by balloon. Three of us took our wives or partners for these first few days, so we were accompanied by my wife Anne, Dick Hamp's wife Toni and Leo Dickinson's partner.

We took the opportunity to explore the area which is steeped in African and British colonial history. The Sudan is the largest country in Africa and its capital is built on the confluence of the White and Blue Nile. The Arabs call this 'the longest kiss on earth' as both great rivers split into two, continuing across some of the most remote and little known regions of the continent.

Khartoum is a fascinating place, formerly ruled by the British until the uprising in January 1885, when Major General Charles Gordon was killed on the steps of the Governor General's palace.

From that historical event the relief of Khartoum began, when Lord Kitchener was ordered by Queen Victoria to take back what was then regarded as British territory. Kitchener built the railroad that still exists today, to carry troops and equipment in order to wage a one-sided war against the Mahdi. His Lordship had transported the army and equipment on the Nile, negotiating the six cataracts of the River Nile. This was no mean feat as it entailed carrying all of the equipment over the unnavigable sections of the cataracts, into the deeper waters of the Nile.

The main line railroad runs from Wadi Halfa, on the Egyptian border, to Khartoum and southwest to Al Ubayyid. The leader of the opposing anti-colonial forces was called The Mahdi and he headquartered in Omdurman, a town across the river from Khartoum. This was where the leader based the 'Mahdi army' and ran his campaign from a grand mud house, which still existed in 1979 and was a museum that photographically recorded the war, with artefacts of the fighting and several letters between Queen Victoria and Major General Gordon. I remember Anne and me spending some time in The Mahdi's house, feeling a little ashamed of some aspects of our glorious military history.

The battles in this campaign are well recorded and none better, in my view, than in Winston Churchill's book, The River Wars, that recalls his involvement in 'the relief of Khartoum', during which took place the last cavalry charge in British military history. You do get the impression that Mr Churchill enjoyed every minute of this bloody episode that was to shape him into the greatest inspirational political leader of the twentieth century.

All of the equipment was being prepared for the journey north and permissions to move, with a section of Sudanese soldiers, through several districts were being collated. Meanwhile, we explored, including the famous Omdurman camel market where the people travelled hundreds of miles in order to trade their animals. There were thousands of camels bought and sold in a precise but undecipherable manner in a general wall of wailing sounds emanating from the buyers, sellers and camels. I was offered one hundred camels in exchange for Anne and I bartered a little to drive up the price but was unable to reach a suitable settlement.

I did get her to ride on a camel, though, which turned out to be rather amusing. Rob Jones and I helped Anne mount into the saddle, at the rear of which sat the owner. This had not been planned so Anne was not really dressed for the occasion and sitting aside the camel revealed a little too much leg. I think the owner saw this as an invitation to have a good rummage and his hands seemed inextricably attracted to her groin area, despite Anne's protestations. Rob and I did what any English gentlemen would do and turned our back sniggering while Anne fought this randy old guy off.

In the end she yelled, 'Michael!' (she always calls me Michael when she is angry with me), so I moved in and yanked the owner's jalabiya and he instructed the camel to get down on his front knees, from which position Anne unceremoniously dismounted.

Khartoum is one of the most fascinating and yet silliest places on this good earth. The local taxis were in a terrible condition. Almost without exception, they had no lights, the glassless reflectors merely painted silver at the front and red for the tail lights. You often had to push them to start and one taxi we climbed into had no floor in the rear. We had to travel holding our legs up in order to make sure we did not make contact with the road below us. Nevertheless, it was a place that was easy to fall in love with. The people, despite the obvious and insurmountable hardships, were kind, generous, warm and welcoming. That did not stop them trying to rip us off at every available opportunity, but they did it with a smile and a thank you.

The food was not great so I treated Anne to a meal at the new Hilton Hotel where I met the former England football manager Don Revie. He had fallen out of favour with the British public and had left the country after resigning his post to manage the Saudi national football team and was visiting Khartoum for an international match against the Sudanese. He wished me good luck with the meal with a knowing smile. It should be all right, I thought. It is the Hilton!

When the vegetable soup arrived, it tasted great but I did find a cigarette end floating in it and called the waiter over. He apologised profusely and grabbed a spoon and fished it out, leaving the soup there for me to finish. You just had to roll with it. The main dish arrived with the used match that had obviously lit the cigarette, floating in the gravy that was poured over what could loosely be described as a steak.

Anne left town with some wonderful memories of her short trip and we prepared to head out into the desert.

Some of our team were already going down with 'tummy troubles' and Liz was kept busy handing out Imodium tablets. We did not know if it was the food or the local beer, appropriately named Camel. It was not good and was sometimes served with a film of oil-like substance floating in it. Notwithstanding that, we drank copious amounts of the stuff, saving the Banks's until we were out on our journey across the Sudan. That was for our planned Monday night sessions, drinking British beer, as we did in the UK.

We piled into two Land Rovers and, with the equipment loaded on the trucks, headed north. It was a nightmare journey over sand tracks. Major Mahrdi explained that the drivers were very knowledgeable and did not need maps to navigate their way across the bush and into the desert. The first night, as we made camp, we realised that we were lost and the drivers had brought us back in a circle to the outskirts of Khartoum.

In the meantime Rob Jones had got quite ill and no amount of Imodium was stemming the flow. We gave him lots of water and started off the following morning. Every time we stopped Rob would walk off with the camp shovel to find a private place to complete his ablutions in a bushy area. As the day past, the bushes got less available and he would just walk a suitable distance and perform. By the end of the day he was so weak, he would just fall out the back of the Land Rover and squat, devoid of all strength and inhibition. Liz, being the only girl and drinking a lot of water, would also look for a bush to go behind, but they were now difficult to find. She would resort to walking several hundred yards away to crouch behind the smallest bush. We did, however, have some big camera lenses and got some great pictures.

We finally arrived, exhausted, at the most northerly point we could get to and made camp. We had been allocated a section of elite Sudanese soldiers by the government to protect us on our journey into little known areas. They were fully armed and would stand guard throughout the night wherever we made camp. We had camp beds but the soldiers scorned them and told us in broken English that the beds were not necessary.

The soldiers were an odd lot and were mildly stoned most of the time. They prepared a substance of mashed herbs, nuts and plants, wrapped in a leaf, and packed it into the space between the lower lip and gums. It was called Pan and they continually sucked it through the lower teeth, extracting a juice and regularly spitting out a brown substance. It was not a pleasant habit. Each night they simply dug a shallow body sized grave-like hole and Major Marhdi explained that the desert was very cold at night but the sand beneath the surface would retain the heat and keep us warm. So we all threw our sleeping bags in and slept under a stunning Sahara sky, watching shooting stars and the Milky Way turn slowly above us in breathtaking clarity. Rob remarked that our dugouts were looking like graves and he slept with a large knife at his side. Even though we were very tired and had eaten our rations, sleep did not come easily.

After a couple of hours, Rob, who was billeted next to me, said, 'Mike, where is the moon?'

I looked over to my left and pointed to it, low on the horizon. 'There,' I said, noticing that the soldiers had started rising from the dugouts talking excitedly.

'Well,' Rob retorted, 'what's that then?' pointing at an orange glowing circular disk shimmering low in the opposite horizon. I had no idea what it was but the locals were now running around our camp scraping at the sand with their feet. We had no comprehension of what was happening. They started shouting 'Train! Train!'

It became immediately apparent that there was, indeed, a train heading straight for us and they were looking for the tracks that were concealed underneath a thin layer of sand. We all ran around in complete panic as the train came closer, not knowing if it was going to plough straight through our camp.

Thankfully, the track, constructed by Lord Kitchener's army, was located some 20 yards from our camp and the speeding train, with a sand plough on the front and hundreds of Sudanese hanging on the side, slowly thundered past us. Rob remarked that when he considered the dangers of this trip, which included lions, hostile tribes, snakes, crocodiles and dysentery, he had never included the possibility of getting run over by a train.

The next morning, Friday January 26 1979, we prepared for the first flight in the Sudan. We laid out the balloon in a sandy hollow near to the village of Ed Debba. The locals crowded around the balloon as it lay, uninflated, in the sand. They had not seen such a thing before and did not know what to expect. Try as we might we could not get them to clear the area so I had the idea of opening the burners. I told Leo what I was going to do and he started the camera rolling. From the basket I ignited both of the burners with an explosion of heat and sound. It scared them instantly and they literally jumped and ran screaming, leaving their sandals behind. It is a very funny part of the documentary 'Diving Over the Desert', which was the new title of the adventure film that Leo Dickinson was filming for Harlech television. It was to be a documentary story of the first crossing of the Sudan by a hot air balloon, warts and all, by a group of ballooning eccentrics. A very British endeavour!

Some aspects of hot air ballooning, particularly when flying in light winds and fine weather, can be a slow paced and potentially boring affair for the camera. I lifted off the ground with Richard Barr and we flew over the villages to the wonderment of the inhabitants, gently floating over the rich vista of the Sahara before climbing to an altitude of 2,000 feet, in order to give the retrieve crew time to reach us. We had ground to air radios and were quickly informed that getting the retrieve crew anywhere near us was difficult and slow going. This first flight was recorded in my pilot's log book as 'Difficult retrieve', a lot of them were. We were often left in the desert for hours; sometimes well into the night while the trucks made their way to us.

While waiting, we used the burners as a light beacon so they could navigate their way along tracks, over sand dunes and lava rock flows. It could take hours and we often got back to the camp very late, cold and tired.

The army food rations were a great success but Chris Beal, our ex-army logistics expert, was not too keen on wasting too much time eating. His preference was to empty all of the rations into one large pot and warm them up. Everything would go in at once, eggs, bacon, soup and pudding. He said it saved time and effort.

The balloon flying was unbelievable in the beautiful African sky. Leo Dickinson got some wonderful footage with our parachute team consisting of Leo and David jumping from the basket, skydiving and linking up while filming with helmet-mounted cameras and often landing in remote places where white men had not been seen before, let alone balloons.

Most of the tribes we met were friendly and welcoming, but on one occasion in northern Sudan we were greeted by a very unfriendly lot. They seemed to think they owned the sky and that we needed their permission to fly. We had landed our balloon near their village and were immediately surrounded by villagers armed with spears and shields, looking very intimidating indeed. We were told by a missionary, coincidentally visiting the area, that this particular tribe were very fierce and could not procreate due to some questionable diseases they had contracted. So they would raid local villages and steal the children.

They were not keen for us to leave the village, particularly after Leo had decided to cool himself down and wash the dust off by jumping into the village watering hole, which they used for drinking water. I came up with a deal, translated to them by Major Marhdi. We would ask the expedition 'doctor' to heal the sick in return for which we would get free passage out of the village. We set up the medicine chest underneath a tree and treated the entire population of the village, giving Aspirin for headaches, iodine for cuts and putting antiseptic cream on the odd abrasion. It was amazing how these fierce warriors were turned into timid puppy dogs, wincing at the sting of the iodine and creams that we applied to their sensitive areas. It worked fine and we went on our merry way towards Merowe and to fly amidst the little known Sudanese pyramids.

Built long after the Great Egyptian Pyramids of Giza, these pyramids were the royal tombs of the kings and queens of Meroe. The burial stones were hewn out of the bedrock and the pyramids were constructed over their remains. The dynasty was thought to be particularly barbaric and on the death of a king, all of his servants were slain or buried alive to look after him on his journey to the next life.

It is said that if a king, during his lifetime, lost a limb or an eye then the servants would suffer the exact same injury. Apparently the logic behind this was so that the servants would ensure that the king remained healthy and fit for fear of the same fate being inflicted upon them. The pyramids were little known and rarely visited due to their remote location.

We flew around the pyramids, making several flights and collecting some great film footage. Leo climbed to the top of one of the ancient structures and I flew past him, almost knocking him off before landing in the soft sand dunes. It became apparent that the trucks carrying the balloons and equipment were not that efficient at coping with retrieving the balloons across this sandy terrain and we seemed to spend many hours in the hot sun, digging out the trucks, so we switched to a more traditional mode of transport – the camel.

We needed to cross a wide section of desert sand dunes so negotiated with a group of camel owners to take the balloons, equipment and our group across this particularly difficult area. It worked well. The camels got used to the balloons and would stand up, unprompted, when we started to lay out the balloons. They were very noisy and seemed to object vocally to almost any prospect of them having to set to work, with a loud rasping, coughing sound that emanated from deep inside the belly and roared out of the mouth. They also drooled a lot with huge festoons of saliva permanently hanging from their lips. They were good to ride though, with their gait producing a gentle and relaxing movement that sent me to sleep.

One day three camel owners stopped and refused to go any further until we had renegotiated the agreed price. There was very little we could do about it as the alternative was to be dumped in the middle of nowhere with no way of getting out. However, it was a memorable time and I treasure a photograph of the expedition walking into the sunset on camel back.

We were able to move back to using the trucks and Land Rovers as we moved to an area call Dinder on the border of Ethiopia which was bush country, as opposed to desert, and camped in a small village, sleeping in traditional grass topped huts. There was game running in the area and we saw our first lions and cheetahs as we flew over typical African grasslands. After breakfast one morning, I took the shovel out of the camp and retired to a wooded area to take care of my ablutions. While I was squatting, with my trousers around my ankles, I was confronted by a troop of very angry baboons. They are fearsome and came at me screaming and wailing and I have to say I had little trouble completing the task for which I had entered the woods. I took the Browning 9mm semi-automatic pistol from its holster at my side. They were unrelenting in their efforts to remove me from their territory and I gathered myself together and slowly retreated to the camp with the troop following some 20 yards behind me. Rob Jones recalls the event well as he was standing with Giles when I came into the clearing with the baboons following me.

Apparently Giles said, 'Well Rob, it looks like our leader is about to get shagged.'

The expedition was moving back towards Khartoum now before making its way south where the population changed from prominently Arabic to black African.

I had been bitten by a large spider, twice, on the neck and was getting very ill. We were sitting in the back of the truck when the spider first bit me and I can still recall the event in slow motion. As Rob saw the spider on my neck and heard me yelp from the sting, he sprang towards me to knock it off, but it bit me again close to the jugular vein and it was extremely painful. We did not recover the spider but I don't think it was venomous and was probably a dirty camel spider. Nevertheless, it did poison me and the inside of my eyelids became ulcerated for two days and I lay under a bush unable to open my eyes. I did not like spiders before this experience. I am paranoid about them now.

We flew every day determined to make a good film and practiced a parachuting stunt that we hoped would be written into aviation history books. We would often arrive in an area to make camp very late, and one night turned up at the edge of a village, dirty and exhausted, at two o'clock in the morning. We made camp in what looked like open ground, erected our camp beds and collapsed into them yearning for sleep. In the morning we awoke to find we had camped in the middle of what was the village abattoir. There were goats' heads and entrails all around us and the smell was terrible. The soldiers, who would not eat any of the rations we were carrying, did not mind this at all. They negotiated the purchase of a goat from the villagers and slit its throat in front of us. We watched it cough itself to death, spewing copious amounts of blood in its final moments. Several of the team found this difficult to handle and it did cause a bit of a rift in the camp.

We had been two weeks in the desert and had all lost weight and were contemplating a nice cold shower and some decent food as we entered Khartoum again. Dick Hamp had left £500 in cash in his room, which he did not discover until we were three days out, and we were all taking bets on the chances of retrieving the money. The expedition money was spread out between us, as a safety precaution, but this possible loss of cash would be a big blow. When we entered the hotel room I immediately enquired at reception if anyone had handed this money in. The response was negative and I was advised to ask the floor boy on level three where our rooms were located. Each floor at the hotel had a floor boy that stayed at the lift to assist guests.

We were astonished when the lift door opened and, recognising us, the floor boy sprang to his feet holding an envelope in his hand and said, 'Mr Mike, your friend left this money.' £500 was a great deal of money in 1979 and represented 5 years of this lad's salary, but he could not steal it. He was poor and honest as so many of the Sudanese people are.

We celebrated in style that night in the bar of the Sudan Hotel, drinking huge amounts of the local Camel beer. We had not drunk beer for a couple of weeks as the Monday night plan to drink the Banks's beer had backfired. Someone had left the large party cans of beer in the fridge on the truck while in transit and the journey across the bumpy roads and track had trashed the fridge.

We had met a chap called Jimmy Mynet from Wolverhampton, who was working in Khartoum. He was an old friend of Rob Jones and he joined us for a night's drinking session. It all got a little out of hand and we started throwing beer around. I was playing a beat up old piano and we were all singing rugby songs when Jimmy slipped on the wet floor. His feet went up in the air and he hit the concrete, chin first, breaking his front teeth and opening his chin to the bone. We all sobered up very quickly. Jim was bleeding badly, holding the flap of skin together as best as he could. We realised that he needed hospital treatment immediately and Major Mhardi suggested we take him to the military hospital.

Jimmy kept repeating, 'Don't let them give me an injection,' aware of the obvious dangers of dirty needles in an Aids- infested Africa.

We got to the hospital and walked up the steps on to a veranda on which was placed a bed with a light bulb over it which I assumed was a place for the hospital guard to rest. We walked through the doors to meet a male nurse who inspected the injury and declared that it would need stitching.

'I'm not having an injection,' hissed Jimmy. He looked at me and said again, 'Don't let them give me an injection.' The nurse told us to take him to the operating area, which turned out to be the old bed outside, and we held Jimmy's arms down while the nurse stitched him up. He was left with a roughly stitched chin which was very lumpy but at least the bleeding was curtailed. I asked the nurse if the lumps would go down and he told me they would not and didn't really understand why it mattered. In time Jimmy returned back to the UK for some plastic surgery and two new front teeth. It was a great night.

Before moving out of Khartoum, to continue our ballooning across the Sudan, we went out for a night to Gordon's nightclub, taking our own bottle of Johnny Walker whisky. We heard that the scotch served at Gordon's was purported as being very poor gut rotting stuff and the management didn't mind if you took your own supply as long as you paid a cover charge. We crowded into three taxis, none of which had any lights and two of which we had to push start. We were stopped on the way by armed police who questioned our movements, but let us carry on after stealing the bottle of Johnny Walker that Giles was holding. The nightclub was a seedy place attended by local and foreign prostitutes as well as a lot of ex-pats. Richard Barr, ever the country gentleman, got into conversation with a local bishop and extended an invitation for him to pass by the hotel and try a single malt that he had brought with him from the UK. We saw this as an opportunity for a prank and we took back a singularly unattractive Irish prostitute who we planted in Richards's room, sitting her on his bed, cross legged and naked.

Apparently Richard took it in his stride when he entered the hotel bedroom. Both he and the Bishop simply said, 'Good evening madam,' and then quietly retired to the veranda to relax on the cane chairs to imbibe in pleasant conversation.

We moved south towards bush country which offered a very different form of flying, with thorn bushes, hilly terrain and much more game. Now we were flying at higher altitudes to practice for the parachuting stunt of skydiving out of a balloon and getting back in it before the diver or the balloon hit the ground. Our flights would often go to above 10,000 feet to give the jumpers enough height to try out the manoeuvres necessary to perform this stunt. This would mean that the balloons were in a lot faster winds and it was impossible for the retrieve crews to get to them. There were long waits in the hot sun, for the pilots and skydivers, with lots of animals around so we had to stay close to the basket and watch each other's back. On one particular flight I spotted a herd of zebra below me and put the balloon into a rapid descent from 4,000 feet, turning the burners on at the last minute, before rounding out of the descent at shoulder level to the zebra. It was a unique moment, the zebra started running and as the wind was quite fast on the surface, I kept with them – right in the middle of the herd – until they simply outran me. Again, another treasured memory and cherished photographs.

It became apparent that the soldiers accompanying us were getting restless as we moved further south, with stories of fighting emerging, and we woke up one morning to see that they had left camp with all of our equipment. Everything had gone, including our rations. We were only two days drive out of Khartoum and close to a local village, built in Arabic style mud hut dwellings. Even in these remote places lorries and trucks did get through with supplies and all we could hope for was that one would come along and take us back to Khartoum. The village head-man took us all to his guest quarters and decided that we needed feeding.

When the food arrived it looked revolting and not one of my team would try it. I did not want to offend this man who could help us get back to the city, so I could not refuse the food. The main dish was a shallow tray filled with what looked like green slime, with lumps in. The head-man put his fingers in the tray and pushed the lumpy bits towards me, indicating that I should use a piece of the accompanying unleavened bread to pick these choice pieces up and eat them. I dipped in a piece of bread and grabbed a lumpy bit and lifted it in the direction of my mouth. It was attached to a glutinous mass of what reminded me of the saliva that drooled in globules from the camels' mouths. I tried to shake of some of this green covered snot-looking substance and popped it into my mouth resisting gagging. I don't know what I was eating but it did not taste nice. I nodded approvingly at the team, who were staring at me wide-eyed, determined that they would join in. They would have none of it, but did eat the bread. This meal, I hasten to add, was washed down with murky well water.

The Sudanese are incredibly warm and generous people and, although poor, would often kill one of the two chickens they possessed in order to feed us and make us welcome at their village. It was always a humbling and levelling experience.

The team met to discuss our predicament. We had no food and our possessions were all gone. Somehow we had to get back to Khartoum. David Howerski, the ex-special services man, suggested that he 'walked out', heading for Khartoum, with one other team member to try and get help. I agreed and we sent him on his way with Richard Barr, loaded with as many water bottles that we could find. The rest of the team were to wait at the village.

We waited there for two days until, by chance, a lorry carrying supplies for the village came to the rescue. I quickly negotiated a price with the driver and we clambered on board bound for Khartoum, concerned for the welfare of David and Richard. We eventually pulled up to the Sudan hotel to find them, looking dirty and dishevelled, both drinking beer on the terrace having arrived an hour before us.

It transpired that the soldiers who had deserted us, having been away from their families for many weeks, had heard that fighting had started in the south and had gone to take some supplies to their families including the very scarce and important commodity, charcoal, used universally for cooking. They had every intention of returning to us, eventually, which they did without a moment of regret or explanation, having satisfied themselves that their families now had enough charcoal to last them through the oncoming troubled times.

With the soldiers, trucks, Land Rovers and all of the equipment now back under our control we moved south again towards the vast area called The Sud. All of our equipment was covered in black dust as they had simply loaded the charcoal on top of it. But we were back on track and about to try to record the final film sequence that we were all so keen to finish.

The balloon was fitted with a rope ladder hanging from the basket where Leo would be positioned for this flight. The plan was to go to altitude with David Howerski in the basket. He would be fitted with a camera mounted on his helmet. He would leave the basket at 12,000 feet falling past Leo, both cameras running. The balloon would be put into a fast descent until it caught up with David and he and the balloon would continue descending at 650 feet per minute. David would fly around the still descending balloon and get back into the basket. At that point Leo would jump off the rope ladder and descend to the ground under his parachute. It would be the first time anyone had jumped out of an aircraft and landed back on it!

It almost went to plan. After exiting the basket at 16,000 feet, the balloon descended and was level with him at 8,000 feet. Both balloon and parachutist were now descending at the same rate of 650 feet per minute. David was unable to get back into the balloon so elected to land on the rope ladder and climb up. It was a very dangerous stunt for both the parachutist and the balloon crew. One mistake by David would have meant him losing his parachute in a tangle on the ladder. We had no idea of the effect of a sudden weight, that of David hitting the balloon, would have as no one had ever done this before. Things were becoming critical, especially as we were getting closer to the ground.

In the end, David flew around the balloon a few times, while filming, and did get safely on to the ladder at 6,000 feet. At the same time Leo jumped away from the rope ladder he was hanging onto. However, David was not able to climb back into the basket and we had no choice but to land the balloon with him still attached, some 20 feet below the bottom of the basket, dangling most precariously on the rope ladder.

It was tricky but we managed to land without incident. We did not manage to find Leo that night. Apparently he had seen some smoke as he was descending under the parachute canopy and headed for it, assuming he would make some human contact. The tribesman tending the fire was terrified by this man coming from the sky, threw a spear at him and ran away. Leo spent the night in a tree until we rescued him the following morning.

We had come very close to a disaster though. On examining the envelope we discovered that the lines holding the parachute rip in place had melted. They were seconds away from breaking which would have left the balloon and crew looking at a catastrophic failure.

We finally ended up in Juba, near the Ugandan border, when the shooting war became a reality and it was obvious that the expedition was over and we needed to get out of that part of the country. The government supplied a military Hercules aircraft and we quickly piled on all of the equipment and the 13 members of our team, flying back to Khartoum with the President, who had also apparently decided that Juba was an unhealthy place in which to stay.

It had been a wonderful, hard, frustrating and exhilarating eight week trip and the sort of life experience that makes lasting memories, but it was time to go home. Befittingly, the journey back was not without some moments of amusement. Chris Beal had lost his return ticket, a fact he announced when he turned up at the airport. He was dressed, for some unaccountable reason, in a large black hat and cloak. I thought I was going to be faced with buying an expensive ticket but he somehow managed to get on board, apparently walking to the plane through a hole in the perimeter fence and boarding the aircraft while no one was looking. Security was not a sophisticated procedure in the Sudan.

Meanwhile I was trying to get the customs officials to take my gun and ammunition and place it in the care of the pilot, which was the established protocol when we had arrived in Khartoum. I spoke to the customs official who told me this would be a process undertaken by his boss. We walked around the circular building looking for his boss and then discovered that he had gone off duty early and would not be returning that day. After discussing this problem for over an hour, with the aircraft to Heathrow boarding, I suggested that I should take the gun and ammunition myself and simply hand it to the pilot. The official considered that and with the passing of several Sudanese pounds, considered it a 'Good idea'.

So I mounted the steps of the aircraft and waved goodbye to the Sudan with a Browning 9mm semi-automatic pistol and 400 rounds of ammunition in my hand.

Chapter Nine

Flying Pints and Thermal Airships

We were met at London's Heathrow by the press, which had been following our exploits in the Sudan and had run stories about our escapades. I had managed to get the telex to connect to my UK office several times during the trips to the Sudan Hotel in Khartoum, and I guess the PR and photo journalism side of me was instinctive. The stories were published in the national papers and had created a lot of interest.

I did a lot of national radio, TV and press interviews and was regularly asked to make after dinner speeches. One American group paid me to fly to New York and speak at the world famous Sardi's – a beautiful Continental restaurant located at 234 West 44th Street (between Broadway and Eighth Avenue) in the Theatre District of Manhattan and a hot place for the very rich and very famous. It was known for hundreds of caricatures of show-business celebrities that adorn its walls. This was an all expenses paid gig with first class tickets and a £500 fee. I landed in New York, went straight to the restaurant, made the speech and got the next plane back, not bothering to stay overnight.

I was anxious to return to the UK to take delivery of my first special shaped balloon. I had gone back to Peter Murdoch, the publicity manager of Wolverhampton-based Banks's Brewery and he had convinced his management board to commission a flying pint balloon, representing the fine ale that was sold through the brewery's 4,000 pubs in the Black Country and beyond. I had presented Peter with some artwork, an artist's impression of what the balloon would look like. It was a pint pot, complete with a handle and a 'good frothy head'. It included a barrel-shaped basket from which we would serve passengers with draught pints of Banks's bitter during flights. I even managed to secure a special registration G-PUBS, the G denoting that it was a British aircraft, Papa, Uniform, Bravo, Sierra from the British Civil Aviation registration desk, which added the final touch. The plan was to use the balloon at pub openings, an idea which was met with great enthusiasm by my crew. We always looked for Banks's pubs after a flight, following one memorable evening debrief when we discovered the Lion O' Morfe, near Claverley.

We had taken off on a local flight from the Bridgnorth Golf Club during a beautiful summer's evening in perfect weather, drifting over the woods, dipping the baskets in every piece of water we could find and generally enjoying ourselves. Dipping the basket in water was a favourite activity for balloon pilots, they could demonstrate their incredible flying skills by placing the basket on top of the water, just enough to get the basket floor wet, as the balloons travelled across lakes or along rivers. If you miscalculated then the basket would fill up and we would all get wet. Very embarrassing. Rob Jones and Pete Mathews were in the basket, taking turns to fly on this idyllic evening when we passed over a building at about 200 feet. There was a car park with several cars on it, including a Rolls Royce, and 20 people looking up at us. All though we were all local, we did not know that this country lane contained a pub.

I leant over the basket and shouted, 'Is this a pub?' and when I received an answer in the affirmative I asked, 'Is it a Banks's house?'

'It is!' a few replied in unison and we immediately opened the rip panel to land in the adjacent field, next to the car park.

The Lion O' Morfe was a traditional country ale house, with real log fires, real ale and frequented by real local characters. The Roll Royce belonged to James Edwards, one of the many gentlemen farmers in the area, but the Land Rovers and tractors in the car park were owned by a clientele that represented a real cross section of the community. There were some outstanding characters, including a chap called Mick whom I never saw sober, even at opening times. He had a rasping, guttural voice that was almost impossible to understand. He would not bother to go to the gentlemen's toilets, preferring to wet himself where he stood, which was usually at the bar. He was normally thrown out at the wetting stage by Bill or Dinah Evans, who ran the pub, and one of the farmers would load Mick into the back of a Land Rover to drop him off at the hay barn, where he slept. The Lion O' Morfe became our watering hole for many years to come.

I was contacted by Ian Phillips, a friend of mine whose neighbouring pub in Newport, Shropshire, was also the local drinking establishment of rock legend Ozzy Osbourne. Ozzy, who lived locally in the village of Ranton, had recently split from his band Black Sabbath and liked the idea of flying in a hot air balloon, particularly a flying pint of Banks's! Ian asked if I would take Ozzy on a flight and I readily agreed. We arranged to meet at the Bell pub in Tong, which was a Banks's house with a large field located next to it. On this particular day the directors of the brewery assembled for the event with Ozzy and his then wife, Thelma.

The flying conditions were good, which they needed to be when flying special shaped balloons. The problem with individual shapes is that as soon as you move away from the classic inverted tear drop design of an aerostat the flying characteristics change drastically. Even though the Banks's balloon was close to the shape of a traditional balloon, it flew very differently. The envelope would easily distort if you ascended or descended at more than 1,000 feet per minute and the handle of the pint mug would create problems, being sensitive to wind shear and acting as a giant rudder by spinning the balloon around.

I well remember a flight over Wolverhampton in this balloon when, in turbulent conditions, the envelope became so distorted that the handle, which was positioned half way up the balloon, came to meet me in the basket. If the basket had threaded itself through the handle the envelope would have lost all of the hot air. It did not bear thinking about. The barrel-shaped basket also presented some difficulties for the landing as the circular bottom gave minimal contact area with the ground upon hitting terra firma, which meant a longer drag across the field. The basket, being the shape it was, also wanted to roll across the field which was disconcerting for the passengers and awkward for the pilots trying to stop it.

Ozzy had arrived in bright yellow trousers and I wondered what colour they would be after this flight. He had just opened Ozzy's Wine Bar in Newport and, by his quiet demeanour, I rather thought he had been in that establishment for most of the day before arriving in the field at 1800 hours for his first hot air experience. Once I had completed the inflation, Thelma, a very pretty and slightly built young lady, declined the invitation to fly, so Ian got into the basket followed by Ozzy. I briefed him on the take off procedure but he was more interested in the on board supply of beer and where we kept the glasses.

We lifted off, without incident, and I looked at Ozzy's hands gripping the rope handles very tightly. This was always an indication of the nervousness of passengers. If their knuckles were white, they were gripping very tightly which showed an emotion somewhere between nervous and terrified. I talked to him and he became more relaxed as the beauty of the countryside unveiled itself below him and the stillness and smoothness of the flight became apparent. From then on, leaning back with an arm on the basket rim and a pint in his hand, he did not shut up for a second.

The flight took us on a heading 15 degrees east of north, flying over the Weston Park estate and into Staffordshire, landing near the sleepy village of Blymhill, after a flight duration of one hour and fifteen minutes. The flight path had taken us towards the area in which Ozzy lived so we landed in a field close to a farmhouse and decided to make our way to his local pub, the Red Lion at Sutton. It was a Banks's house but, to be fair, we had little choice since it was one of the few pubs that Ozzy had not been banned from.

It was one of the funniest and most riotous nights of my life. On the way to the pub he told me the story of his break-up with his band

and his determination to go ahead with his solo career, a decision that history shows was correct. We elected a driver and then proceeded to drink our way into a giggling stupor. Ozzy is a great storyteller and was recounting his visit to the USA where they, as Black Sabbath, toured the country using an old Dakota aircraft to fly the band to gigs. I was planning to embark on a flight to the edge of space which Ozzy found amazing and explained his encounter with zero G or weightlessness while flying in the Dakota. Apparently the pilot of this ancient aircraft was always attired in a grey mackintosh and black beret and was obviously a little eccentric. He flew the band to gigs across America, always extolling the virtues of this fine old aircraft. He had told them it was possible to attain weightlessness by flying in an arc, at which time you entered zero gravity for a short time. The band told him they were up for it and as they went over the arc, the band floated away in different directions in the fuselage. Ozzy described this in the pub, demonstrating a sort of breast stroke action in an effort to retrieve his can of Budweiser that was floating some distance away from him and trying to avoid the floating ball of vomit that was launched from the drummer during this stomach-churning event.

Ozzy had a natural comedic presentation to his stories and he described a gig in Australia where the fans were separated from the stage by a water-filled moat. He was performing on stage, wearing a heavy lamé cloak and boots with four inch cork heels. He told of the moment he spotted a large-breasted blonde fan hanging over the moat edge with her breasts almost touching the water and he jumped into the moat to swim over to her. Impressive! Except for the fact his cloak held his head under the water while his boots held his feet on the surface.

'I kept coming up and screaming, "Help!" but they just screamed back, "YEAH! YEAH!" I was fucking drowning.'

Apparently he managed to grab the side wall of the moat and surfaced right where the blonde girl was positioned. He immediately collected his thoughts, tried to act as cool as a Prince of Darkness should and said to the young lady, 'Hiya Honey, want to come back to my dressing room?' He was out of breath, half drowned with his make-up running. Not an attractive look for a rock star.

The blonde looked at him and said, 'Oh fuck off, you fat sod!'

He added, 'I felt a right prat.' Ozzy does have this self-deprecating sense of humour, always delivered with a glint in his eye and a pint in his hand.

Since this flight I have not been in direct touch with Ozzy but have been told that he has no recall of the flight and believes it was some sort of substance-enhanced hallucination, dream or nightmare.

He has since claimed in some biography or article, 'I was in the sky, drifting around in a fucking pint of bitter, standing in a barrel, drinking beer and looking down on the earth. Fuck me, man, I don't know what I was on at the time but it must have been fucking good stuff.'

The next time I flew the Banks's balloon it was with a blind passenger. He wanted to experience this form of flight even though he could not see. It was a startling experience for me. Brian could sense every movement of the balloon, no matter how slight. He could detect small changes in height and knew the instant we were going up or down. I was talking to him intensely, describing the views, buildings and animals and if we were flying over a herd of sheep I would tell him and he would say, 'Yes, I can hear them.' If we were flying over a crop he would say, 'Yes, I can smell it.' He explained that he knew if we were going up or down as he was holding one hand outside of the basket rim and if his palm was colder it meant we were falling and if the back of his hand was cooler, we were rising. It was a developed sense of touch that in some way compensated for his inability to see. I tried it myself and it worked. From that time I always flew with my hand held out and the changes became faster and more sensitive than the variometer instrument, which indicated the speed of ascent and descent. Having this extra sensory perception really is an aid to lighter than air flying and I taught all of my students to do this.

I had now started competition flying. This sport is organised by the British Balloon and Airship Club and is a competition to find a British champion who would qualify for a shot at the World Hot Air Balloon Champion title. Competition flying is quite complex and takes many hours of practice. Basically, the pilot has to drop a weighted streamer on to, or as close to as possible, a target which is positioned in a field somewhere by the judging panel. In a 'judge declared goal' you are given the coordinates of where the target cross is located. It is never placed directly downwind, that would be too easy, so the pilot has to use the varying wind directions at different altitudes to steer the balloon to the target. It requires great skill and is highly competitive and cut-throat.

Understanding the many rules and regulations is a task in itself. Many a pilot falls foul of them before he even gets to fly in the competition. Other tasks include the Hare and Hounds, in which a 'hare' balloon takes off some fifteen minutes before the pack of 'hound' balloons are released to follow it. Prior to competing in my first championship Dick Wirth, managing director of Thunder Balloons, signed his recently published book saying 'Sorry I beat you at the championships', which he did, quite easily.

On the next attempt, the following year, I became quite disenchanted with competition flying, unable to cope with the politics or understand the bureaucracy that ran the events. I was flying to a judge declared goal and was the clear favourite to win this task. All of the other competitor balloons were at least a half mile to the right of me as I came to the target and I could see the main group over farm buildings. I dropped my streamer at the target and, with only one balloon within 100 yards of me, I was quite satisfied that I had clearly won this event, by a country mile. There was a protest being made that the judges were to consider under advisement. Apparently, one of the farmers complained that some balloons had scared his cattle and the balloons named were disqualified. I was horrified to see my name on the disqualification list as I was nowhere near the position that was referred to on the complaint. In fact, I could not have been one of the offending balloons as, due to timings, it would mean that I had been in two places at once. I could appeal to the panel of judges, in payment of a fee that was none returnable if the complaint was upheld. As I felt that it was impossible to uphold the complaint, I confidently went before the panel to plead my case. They rejected my claim out of hand and stated that two of the competition flyers had confirmed that I had flown over the complaint area at the time specified.

'Well, they would, wouldn't they,' advised another pilot with a knowing glance.

If the truth was upheld I would be leading the competition and they could not risk that when such an easy option was at their disposal. I expect that I was naive enough to believe in fair play and integrity.

'More fool you,' remarked Dick Wirth, and I decided that I would not partake in these games in the future, preferring to win contracts rather than competitions.

Thunder Balloons merged with Lindstrand Balloons and Dick Wirth and I often sat and pontificated about the future of the industry and the exciting opportunities that were arriving on a daily basis. Dick called me on one occasion and asked to see me about a design for a new airship idea that Per Lindstrand had come up with. He explained that Per had a new thermal airship on the drawing board. Cameron Balloons had a thermal airship which was basically loosely based on a shape similar to a Goodyear blimp, but was filled with hot air. The gondola was attached to the envelope on which were mounted two burners and an engine that drove a propeller to give it forward motion. It was steered by an inflated rudder, operated by lines in the gondola. It took two pilots to fly the machine as the steering, engine speed and burner operation were too much for a single pilot. I had seen this rather ugly flying machine and the weight of the gondola and engine made the envelope sag and look very distorted, resembling a pregnant guppy. It was difficult to inflate in anything other than almost flat calm winds and, from what I had observed, was almost impossible to fly in anything more than 4 knots wind speed. This severely curtailed its operations and, given that the thermal airship was a lot more expensive than a hot air balloon, they would not, in my estimation, represent good value for the client. Hot air balloons were, in any event, reliant on good weather and these contraptions would only make flying more difficult and more expensive. I had decided to keep away from them.

However Dick Wirth presented me with a drawing that looked very good. The envelope was pressured so that its rather nice shape could be maintained. In addition, the steering would be via a centrally mounted joy stick using vectored thrust. The thrust for the steering would be provided by the propeller that would force air down a fabric tube, escaping at the rear of the airship, from either side, when a valve was opened. It sounded perfect and Dick explained that they needed the cash to build the first machine. I quickly found a client to sponsor the endeavour - the manufacturer of the Peter Stuyvesant cigarette brand.

I commissioned the first Lindstrand airship and went to the initial test inflation. It looked amazing, a PR man's dream. Constructed in the rainbow colours of Stuyvesant, its sleek and racy design represented the very latest in lighter than air technology. We took the gondola to several balloon events and the press reported on this new and exciting mode of travel.

However, nothing is ever simple in ballooning and it became obvious that the new and revolutionary vectored air steering system did not work. Lindstrand's were forced to re-design the tail fins, putting on an inflated rudder and two lines to the gondola with which to steer it. Its first flight was set in a blaze of publicity with great footage and pictures, and the new thermal airship rose majestically into the sky on its maiden flight. There was nothing else majestic about it. The two pilots immediately reported to me that they were having difficulty keeping the ship in the air and were unable to steer it effectively.

The last message I got over the radio was, 'We're crashing, we're crashing!' as we raced in the retrieve vehicle to help them.

And crash they did, right into the middle of a housing estate. As we drove along the road we could see the tail of the aircraft poking out above the houses. Some had missing chimneys, cleanly removed by the ship bouncing off roofs as it plunged back to earth. The PR man's dream had turned into the PR man's nightmare, as the press saw the obvious and immediate news value of this incident, taking pictures that appeared the next day under a headline that screamed 'WARNING. CIGARETTES CAN SERIOUSLY DAMAGE YOUR HOUSE!' It was all too painful.

* * *

I was next on my way to Thailand on a Kuwait Airways Boeing 747 with a strange little man whose name I will omit for reasons that will become obvious. I shall refer to him as Jack. The tyre business was becoming an international company with dealers in 12 European countries and we had also begun to manufacture Formula Three racing cars called the Anson. These were designed by a respected racing engineer, Gary Anderson, who currently commentates on Formula One for the BBC.

In order to test the cars and tyres we had to bring through young racing drivers and, to facilitate this, our Swiss Yokohama distributer had negotiated a lease deal with the Grand Prix track in Pattaya, Thailand. The plan was to do all of the testing at that circuit and that meant providing a well-known racing car driving instructor. Jack was that man and we met for the first time at Terminal 3 in Heathrow, in the departure lounge. He was wearing a white jacket with red piping around the lapels, he had grey hair presented in a Bobby Charlton comb-over style and looked like a Walls hot dog salesman who had lost his trolley.

He had not visited Thailand before and was naturally inquisitive about the country, its culture and, above all, its sex industry. I had travelled to Thailand on many occasions and was struck by the influence that the sex industry had on all sections of the culture, communities and its economy. The sex shows in the Patpong area of Bangkok have migrated to all of its cities and beyond to the towns and villages, with young girls being encouraged into the sex trade for the easy money it offered to poor communities. Sadly, this trade dilutes and diverts away from the ancient and colourful traditions of the country's vast and rich history and focuses the tourist attention away from village culture and eastern religion, with its stunning architectural temples and historic trade legacies that lie at the heart of this unique country. The tourists are now pointed towards the sex shows of Bangkok, the ladyboys of Pattaya and the vast community of prostitutes that provide for the seemingly unrequited appetite of the visiting male population. It seems that one of the most diverse cultures on earth is unable to escape from the economic trap that delivers the huge wealth generated from this seedy and ugly business. Even the once famous Thai massage is no longer available from even the highest of star rated hotels, without the offer of a 'happy ending' albeit from some of the most beautiful of young ladies on the planet.

Jack and I walked along the sea front in Pattaya, fascinated at the carousel bars which gently rotated in a full circle so that the tourist could conveniently view the ladyboys that adorned every seat. They were all astonishingly beautiful, elegant and tall with only a prominent Adams apple available to establish the gender. We moved to a large but very smart bar and sat on the balcony overlooking its interior dance floor that was packed with girls, in couples, dancing to exhibit their wares to the many male visitors patrolling the floor.

Jack came up with the inevitable observation, 'They're beautiful aren't they?' adding, 'I've never had a Thai girl before.'

I told him that if he wanted one, he should go down to the floor and get one, but I added that we had to go back to the hotel soon as we needed to be at the racetrack early in the morning.

He dithered nervously for several minutes, telling me he liked one particular girl, 'That one in the leopard skin dress,' he said pointing.

I explained that if he just walked up to her she would understand what he wanted and she would be off with him to the hotel. He asked how much it would cost and we were told by the table waiter that the going rate was 340 Baht (approximately £10). He looked in his pocket and found that he only had 35 Baht – so I gave him the 340 and urged him to get on with it. We needed to go. In the end, with all Jack's vacillation, my patience ran out and he asked me to go down with him. I simply took him across the dance floor, stopped at the girl in question and pushed him forward. The young lady latched on to him immediately and off we went to our hotel.

The next morning I was enjoying a breakfast I always eat in Thailand, a chilli, cheese and mushroom omelette, when Jack joined me looking somewhat dishevelled from, I presumed, lack of sleep. He had obviously not showered and his comb-over was not fully combed over, the left side resting on his shoulder to reveal a shiny and somewhat unattractive bald pate. It was not a look conducive to the modern day stud which the expression on his face was attempting to portray.

'Well, *she* had a good time,' he said, 'I think she has really taken to me.'

'Yes, I'm sure she has,' I replied. 'Can you put her in a taxi, we have to go to the track.' Jack returned some fifteen minutes later, now showered and changed, and I moved towards the taxi that was booked to take us to the racetrack.

'She won't go,' he insisted, 'I think she is in love with me.'

'For goodness sake,' I retorted, 'she's a prostitute. Just pay her and put her in a taxi. We are late!'

'No,' he insisted, 'she does not want to leave me, she is infatuated with me, she just keeps crying and shouting, "more please!"'

I thought that was unlikely, even though his comb-over was now firmly pasted to his head. I made my way, with him, to his room. Sure enough she was crying and shouting, 'No. No, I want more, please!' making a grab for his 65-year-old hand.

'I don't think she's met anyone like me before,' he said, looking smugly into those mascara smudged oriental eyes. I gently took her arm and we put her into a taxi and sent her off on her way.

During the taxi ride to the racetrack he remained convinced that the girl saw him as something quite unique and was obviously proud of the incident and his prowess as a lover and blade. We got to the racetrack and we both fumbled for the fare when he produced the 340 Baht I had given him the previous evening.

'I thought you paid her?' I said.

'Bloody hell,' said Jack. 'I think I gave her the 35 Baht by mistake?'

'You daft old bugger,' I said. 'You've just paid her 10p for a night of sex! No wonder she was crying and shouting, "more please!"'

I left the racetrack with him having promised me he would go back to the bar where she worked and recompense her for her night's toil.

I did have one more meeting before departing and I was dreading it. The last time I went to this particular restaurant the waitresses were giving blow jobs under the table while the guests were reading the menu, deciding upon the main course. The food in Thailand can be sensational, but sometimes the service is a little over the top.

* * *

I did have this feeling that ballooning was a pastime that should be shared by others and I wanted to make it available. It seemed that everywhere I went everyone I spoke to was fascinated by this form of flight. For every person I flew, for the first time, it provided a life changing memory. I took a local performer named Jeff Bodenham on a flight over Shropshire and he promptly wrote a song about what he referred to as, 'A special experience.' I had known Jeff for many years, having been entertained by his singing and story telling at various venues throughout the Midlands. He was a Wolverhampton-born entertainer of great musical and comedic ability and was a teacher at a school in Dudley in the West Midlands. He used his experience teaching the Black Country pupils to recite very funny anecdotes and I produced an album for him named 'In a Class of His Own', full of stories punctuated by a mixture of songs.

On Jeff's flight in the Woolworths balloon, we flew from close to his home in Codsall Wood and headed towards RAF Cosford, the site of the renowned Royal Air Force Museum, dedicated to the history of aviation and the Royal Air Force in particular. The museum is a non-departmental public body sponsored by the Ministry of Defence and a registered charity.

RAF Cosford was also a training base and had an active runway so I needed permission to land or climb to 2,000 feet to overfly its airspace. We still did not carry radios and I could not contact the tower to ask permission to land so I set the balloon down low to the ground so my intentions were obvious to the tower. The tower shone a green light at the balloon which indicated permission for me to land. I levelled the balloon out, at few feet above the ground, with the intention of a touch-down on the grass before the runway. There was a sewage farm on the approach to the airfield and I let the balloon cool down, just a little too much, as we were skimming over it. The leading edge of the basket just caught the slurry for a few yards, disturbing the sewage and creating the most terrible smell before we settled, still fully inflated, on the clean grass of the airfield.

Jeff remarked, 'That was not so much a landing, as going through the motions.' A rather witty remark to end a very pleasant flight. A Land Rover with RAF personnel drove over to us and out jumped a uniformed man and a similarly attired very pretty blonde lady.

'Hi,' the man said, offering his hand to me. 'I'm Corporal Jones but people call me Shag. How can I help?' I explained to Shag that I needed to deflate the balloon and we needed permission to bring the retrieve crew in. He suggested that I fly the balloon over the runway to the other side of the airfield which was close to the main gate and he added with a wink 'which is near the bar.' I agreed to this as it seemed an eminently sensible suggestion, but I would need permission from the controller in the tower. He told me he would handle that but asked if I would give the lovely uniformed blonde bombshell a flight over the airfield. I did not hesitate for long before agreeing to this and the lady in question hitched up her RAF skirt to clamber into the basket, revealing her RAF issue suspenders and stocking tops. I then briefed her fully with special emphasis, as I always did for pretty passengers, on the need to do exactly as the pilot said and not to leave the basket until I gave permission. She was RAF and accepted and fully understood the instruction.

We took off again and I immediately got a red light from the control tower. Shag shouted me to tell me to take no notice so I flew on across the airfield and the young lady explained that Shag would sort it out, adding that he controlled almost everything on this airbase. I remember thinking what a lucky bugger he was.

We flew gently over to the other side of the airfield where the retrieve crew were waiting and, reminding my passenger of the landing brief, I settled the balloon down and immediately pulled the rip line to deflate the balloon after positioning myself, back towards the landing, snugly between the fuel cylinders. The balloon tipped over gently forcing the passenger to lie, face down on top of me, my arms around her in close embrace.

'You sod,' she said. With a huge grin across her lovely face. 'When can I get out?'

'Only when I tell you,' I repeated, 'we have to wait until the balloon is cool, try and keep still.' But she couldn't and went into howls of wriggling laughter. My weak protestations and requests that she kept still made this considerably worse, she knew what I was doing but was uncertain about the effect of ignoring my instruction. In the end she relaxed sobbing with laughter and lay on me in an intimate resignation of the position she found herself in. I finally told her she could leave the basket but asked her to do it gently and would she be careful where she put her knees as she got off me. Ballooning is such good fun!

We packed the balloon away and retired to the bar for a riotous evening, drinking Tiger beer and playing an old piano until the early hours.

I can remember the singer Kiki Dee's first flight with me, from Hagley Hall near Birmingham. Before I put her through the enviable, ladies only, landing process she was totally smitten by the experience, romance and sheer exhilaration of flying above the countryside, suspended in a basket by a balloon. She asked me to marry her (jokingly of course). She sent me a copy of her latest album signed 'Thank you for looking after me, even though you turned me down, Kiki.'

I knew I had to share ballooning with everybody, or provide the opportunity for everyone to experience this extraordinary and exhilarating form of manned flight. I felt that I should renew my efforts to have my balloons flying over some of the great landmarks and stunning vistas that were available in different parts of the world. I had to find the right locations to make this happen and thought of the Ngorongoro Crater in Tanzania. I would go there and take a look.

Chapter Ten

Family Matters

It's a true and inevitable consequence of over 40 years of marriage that my wife Anne and our children have shaped my life to a large degree. They say opposites attract. I am an impulsive person, with a tendency to embroider the odd yarn and have an over-optimistic view of my more adventurous activities that can annoy my family. I have a quick temper, with a gregarious personality that is not slow to recognise and need the approval and support of my peers. I can play to a crowd and I like people to like me.

Anne, on the other hand, is a shy and quiet girl who shuns any limelight, is almost abstemious, could easily die of embarrassment and quietly considers situations – before she tells me I am wrong. This has been good for the family and, fortunately, a lot of her traits have migrated, by example, to my children.

Although optimistic about my own endeavours, I can carry a morbid outlook where others are concerned. If someone close is driving to see us and is late, I immediately assume that they are dead, while Anne assumes they are simply late. She is not at all quick tempered but she is a redhead and on the rare occasions she has lost it, I ducked! She never swears and even when I have been in serious danger she seems to take an analytical, considered and calm approach. The children always look to her expression and reaction in order to gauge how much trouble they or I am in. So I have been fortunate that my children have used their mother as a worry barometer in order to determine whether or not they should enter into panic mode.

My language has always been ripe, much to Anne's annoyance, and try as I might to get her to utter expletives, I have been singularly unsuccessful in that endeavour. She once remonstrated with me for my continued use of the word 'twat'. I explained to her that this was an OK word – a derivative of the words twit and prat, but to my horror she started to use it herself, all the time. I suppose, if it had been a derivative of those words it would, in her mind anyway, be a perfect description of several characters that were arriving late, not finishing jobs on time or not delivering items when they should. That meaning could aptly apply to a surfeit of inefficient and incompetent people that a householder may rely on to provide a stress-free level of domesticity.

However I heard her using this word, on the telephone, to an elderly and treasured friend, Joy Cartwright, who was obviously complaining to Anne about the shortcomings of a particular tradesman that seemed incapable of fulfilling his promised obligations.

'Yes,' I heard Anne say, 'you cannot put up with that, at your age, he is obviously a total twat.' She used the word multiple times during the conversation, on the telephone in our kitchen, and I had to act. I calmly explained to her that the word did not mean twit or prat, or any derivative thereof, and that it was, in fact, a reference to the female genitalia. I will never forget her staring and penetrating expression and I quickly glanced around the kitchen work surfaces because if there had been a knife, she would have stabbed me.

For all this calmness, I have to say that our home is filled with fun and laughter and I do not know anyone that smiles and laughs as much as my wife. She's fun.

So on a particular balloon launch, in the Dinitrol balloon at Weston Park, I had inflated the balloon, watched by Anne and the kids, in blustery conditions in order to fly the client, a Mr Robin Bassett. We had won the contract to operate this balloon some months before but he had never flown in it. Two of my other balloons lifted off without drama as

I loaded my client into the basket. He had one leg in the basket when a gust of wind snatched it out of the crew's hands, sucked up by a large black-looking cloud that had snuck up on me and hurled me into the sky, in a completely opposite direction than the other two balloons.

The ground crew, of course, are not allowed to let their feet off the ground, under any circumstances. That is drilled into them constantly. They will hold the basket down as long as they can but will release it if they are in danger of being lifted. A pilot will always take a quick look over the basket, as the balloon ascends, to make sure no one has hung on. A crew member falling from as low as 30 feet will usually result in a fatality.

So up in the air I went leaving Mr Basset on his backside in the field. The severe gust from the cloud had blown out the pilot lights so I had no operational burner. I was rising very fast but I knew the envelope was not inflated properly and when the balloon had reached whatever height the gust was taking me too, it would fall out of the sky like a stone, unless I put some hot air into the envelope quickly. The envelope did not even look like a balloon at that stage. Rather than an inverted tear shape of a fully inflated envelope, it was more of a pencil shape with a bubble of cold air in the top. I lit the burners but the mouth (opening) was closed and I gently coaxed the burners into action with short blasts, which eventually opened the mouth of the balloon. Once the mouth was fully open I blasted heat from all three burners into the envelope, hoping it was going to be enough. I reached a height of 2,500 feet before the cloud dumped me and I hurtled downwards rapidly. Fortunately, I had caught it in time and after a few minutes the balloon became stable. I looked back at the launch field to wave at the crew, indicating I was back in control, but could not identify where it was. I looked out of the basket a full 360 degrees and could still not identify where I was. I only knew that I was travelling very fast. Too fast. I looked again to see an airfield below me but I knew there should be no airfields in the area. I had absolutely no idea where I was so decided to land immediately, which at this speed was also going to be a challenge. I remembered something that John Gore had told me, during my early test flights, four years had now passed and ballooning had moved forward somewhat. He explained that he was once going so fast that he would not be able to find a field big enough for the drag. He told me that he had put the basket down, close to a downwind field hedge, which acted as a brake as he went through it. Given the circumstances, I decided to give it a try and had my eye on a field 400 yards ahead. I dropped the balloon down to 100 feet at the edge of the first field, noticing a lone bull that looked at me but seemed unperturbed. I suppose if you are a bull you do not need to worry about much in life.

I dumped some air, using the rip line, and eased the balloon into the field very smoothly, but again at great speed. The basket tilted to a 45 degree angle and, as predicted, the envelope turned into a spinnaker and I went sailing across the field until the basket met the hedge. The envelope continued with its momentum and dragged everything through the hedge with me curled up in the bottom, depositing me in the next field as the envelope fully deflated. I inspected the hedge and was surprised that it showed hardly any sign of suffering from this violent assault. I was safe, the balloon undamaged and the bull was not worried at all, with his head peering over to look at what was going on.

I had no idea where I was and walked out of the field to find a farmhouse to inform the landowner and locate the nearest phone. I came across a red telephone box standing alone and situated in the middle of nowhere. Luckily it worked so I could telephone the retrieve number but had no idea where I was and there were no obvious landmarks to refer to. The centre of the dial was missing so I had no reference to give the retrieve crew and I considered ringing the operator or emergency services to determine an approximate location.

However I was rescued and assisted by the appearance of a large red and muddy Massey Ferguson tractor which stopped when I raised my hand and asked the driver where I was.

'You in that balloon thing?' he asked, with the inevitable, 'Where did you come from?'

I informed him of where I had landed and of my predicament. He knew exactly which field the balloon was in and had watched the process, telling me it was his land and to 'watch the bull' as he could be a 'nasty bugger'. He me gave permission to let the retrieve crew into the field, advising me to close the field gate first as the bull had access into both fields. I was glad I had not noticed that.

Having got the name of the nearest village, I called the retrieve number and waited, during which time I studied the map. It was apparent that I had travelled at lightning speed under that cloud. The airfield I had seen from the basket was a disused World War II base near Wheaton Aston and the fact that I got there in minutes frightened me stiff.

The crew arrived with Anne, Myles and James who both leapt out of the car, running towards me. They were obviously concerned and glad to see that I was OK. I could tell they had been anxious and that surprised me, given the calming influence of their mother. I dropped to my knees for a hug of assurance and they asked me if I was alright.

'Of cause I am,' I said, 'absolutely fine, no problem, don't worry.'

James, the youngest by a year said, 'I was all right until mummy looked up and said, "Oh shit!" And I knew something was wrong.'

Anne, of course, merely remarked, 'Well, that was interesting, wasn't it?'

There is no doubt that the flight was a piece of poor judgement on my part. I should have been aware of the threatening cumulous cloud moving too close and the dangers which that presented. The old school balloonists used to say that a new pilot was normally safe for the first 100 hours after check out. At that point over-confidence would kick in and mistakes would be made. I think that was certainly the position that I was in. Hey, I had 100 hours in the log book, been there, done that, worn the T-shirt and was in line to get my precocious bottom smacked.

A similarly dangerous flight took place from our favourite site in Quatford, a village in the Severn Valley. We had selected a field completely surrounded by tall trees, so no matter what the surface level wind speed was, the launch area was calm. We inflated the Woolworths balloon at dawn one morning with a Met forecast of 10 to 15 knots all the way up to 1,000 feet. Being 'experienced sky gods', we knew we were good flyers and more than capable of flying at such speeds, in fact we were so great, we could handle anything. The old adage that 'if you can stand the balloon up, you can take off' rang loudly in our ears, which were receptive only to signals of bravado and compulsion so easily accepted by young impulsive minds. I knew it was windy and took along a trail rope which I had never used since my check out flight.

We took off hot with Rob Jones and Peter Mathews. Rob recalls that flight and says he knew we were in trouble when we rose above the tree line and the wind kicked in. He can remember that the balloon tilted at such an alarming angle, when the wind took hold, he thought he was going to fall out of the basket. I can only remember his stream of panicky expletives over the roar of the burners.

We had calculated a forty-five minutes flight time before faced with the necessity to land before entering Birmingham airspace. I passed the map to Rob, asking him to navigate while Pete kept a look out for animals.

'Sod the map,' Rob hollered and, pointing in the direction we were heading, shouted, 'That's Birmingham. Get this thing on the fucking ground, quick!'

I had little option but to oblige and set the balloon up for a landing in a field full of concrete pig sties. I briefed Pete to throw out the trail rope and Rob wedged himself in the bottom of the basket, gripping my legs to stop me leaving the basket prematurely. It really was horrifyingly fast and an impact with one of the pig sties would definitely not be pleasant. Somehow it worked and we bounced heavily between the concrete structures before slamming to a stop at the end of the field. No injuries, more by luck than judgment. Anne came into the field in her normal unflustered way and handed us bacon sandwiches wrapped in foil, but we were still getting our breath back and felt too sick to eat them.

'I told you it was too windy to fly,' she remarked knowingly and walked off. Cow!

I did experience one situation where I could see Anne concerned and flustered, though.

We had taken the Woolworths balloon to Rhyl, the seaside resort in North Wales. Our brief was to take off from the promenade, in front of the Woolworths store. This was always going to be a difficult flight as the seafront is normally quite a windy location and in the evening, when we were due to fly, you could expect a sea breeze. A sea breeze is a wind coming from the sea inshore. It is caused by the diurnal variation between the cold sea and the warmer land mass. Heat rises from the warm land and is filled by a cool wind from the sea. The problem is that, often, the gradient wind (the wind above 1,000 feet) can be in a different direction to the surface wind. In this case the gradient wind was straight out to sea, but taking off from the promenade, in front of the Woolworths store, was going to need a quick ascent in order to avoid the buildings. So the trick was going to be to take off, level off as soon as possible heading out to sea and then descend to catch the sea breeze which would take us back over the beach front and further inshore.

The deliberation before take off was simply based around the fact that a sea breeze can be eradicated once the heat differential of the land and sea has stabilised. The flight could well leave us facing a possible sea ditching and life boat rescue. The inevitable 'would it, should it' and 'should we, could we' conversation took place and the downside of being stranded with the ignominious possibility of a sea rescue, with all of its inherent dangers, inconvenience and potential costs, were fully debated. All this I conducted with my trainee pilot, Martin Wall, along with the question of the irresponsibility of such an action. It was determined that it would indeed be dangerous and irresponsible to fly in those conditions. So we took off anyway.

We 'popped off' the promenade comfortably avoiding the buildings, rising to 1,500 feet and, as predicted, drifted out to sea to the astonishment of the holiday making onlookers, police and fire brigade. With fingers crossed and buttocks clenched we descended to 500 feet and to our immense relief found the onshore sea breeze about one mile out to sea. We drifted back towards the sea front, hoping that the now favourable wind would stay with us until we met the shore and cleared the town to find a landing spot. I overflew the town a little illegally since air law pronounced that a minimum height of 500 feet should be kept *above* any structure but there was the caveat that exceptions could be made if the aircraft was landing or in some difficulty. I would argue that I was landing and in potential difficulty, although, it has to be said, I had put myself in that position.

Just outside the town there were many fields available and after looking out of the basket and checking that the retrieve crew were visible and close, I chose a large grass field, landed the balloon and deflated the envelope. The crew arrived after getting permission from the farmer and entered the field. We started to pack the balloon. This is a simple process of putting the envelope in as thin a line as possible while a crew member squatted in a kneeling position at the mouth and worked their way up, squeezing the last remaining air out as they go before packing it away in the envelope bag.

A herd of cows had meandered into the field through an open gate in an adjoining paddock. Now cows are curious animals who wanted to see what was going on and about 50 of them decided to inspect the balloon envelope.

Anne said 'I don't like cows,' and pulled the children to her nervously.

'Oh they're all right,' I said, 'but we have to pack this away quickly,' noticing that they were starting to lick the envelope. Cows have rough tongues and can lick holes in balloon fabric.

'I don't like cows,' she repeated as the animals crowded around us. 'And I hate bulls,' she shouted, taking the children and running to safety behind a gate in the nearest hedge. Instinctively, we all followed her and ran out of the field to take refuge. I looked past the cows and saw that the bull, to which Anne was referring to, was slowly walking up to the herd.

'Christ,' Martin remarked, 'it's a bull – and this is a red balloon! It might charge us.'

We calculated that we should have time to pack away the balloon before the bull reached us and frantically and illogically proceeded to do this while Anne, the crew and the children shouted instructions to us but refused to help. Martin was almost under the hooves of the cows when one dopey looking animal who would not move decided to defecate on Martin's head while he was bending over packing in the last of the fabric.

'It's crapped on my head,' he said, with a *help me* look on his face and now appearing like a North Wales farmer wearing a cow pat coloured flat cap. We finished packing and moved back to the safety of the gate to assess the situation with Martin's head looking in a terrible mess, the cow pat now having dried and firmly embedded itself in his hair. He looked funny and helpless. Anne diplomatically suggested we try to find a water trough to dip his head in.

We had been married for eight years and I had no idea she was afraid of cows.

Martin was a good student pilot and acted as crew, in return for which I gave him as many instruction flights as possible. That was the way it worked. The student pilots get a lot of responsibility, it's an important part of the training process but it is the ultimate responsibility of the PIC (Pilot In Command) to make sure the flight is conducted in a safe and legal manner. The pilot has to check and recheck everything. Well they should do.

On one occasion I was flying Bluebird from a show with Martin as pilot under training. We had inflated the balloon but had a long wait in blustery conditions. Martin had done all the flight checks and I reeled off the list to him

I started, 'Parachute rip?'

'Secured,' he replied.

'Fuel?'

'Checked and full,' he confirmed.

'Maps?'

'On board, Mike.'

'Retrieve crew?'

'Briefed,' he returned, and so it went on.

It was a very small launch site with a short distance to the down-wind public gallery. I told him to 'go out hot' and we left the site in a very quick ascent. There was no need to burn at all. I noticed it was rapidly getting colder, so decided not to burn as I did not want to go through the cloud base which was at 4,000 feet, electing to wait for the balloon to cool and make a controlled descent to the nearest field. This was a show flight and it was not going to be very long. The balloon was still rising and we had time to check the maps, wind direction and downwind obstacles or airspace restrictions. We levelled out and I put the balloon into a 500 feet per minute descent. I saw that the fuel level on tank one was reading at below 30 per cent. I went onto tank two and immediately saw the fuel was also on 30 per cent. I checked fuel tanks three and four. They were empty. I asked him if he had checked the tanks and he told me he had.

I will add that the propane tanks had gauges that only indicated fuel quantity below 30 per cent. To check if they were full you needed to open a bleed valve at the top of each tank to check that there was liquid gas at the top of the tank. It was a bad mistake but ultimately my responsibility. I was descending from 3,500 feet with less than a full cylinder of gas. This put a completely different dynamic to the flight. We needed to get down quickly, find a field and land. I knew I would use the thirty percent in tank one on the descent. There were a lot of electricity pylons in the area, which we needed to keep away from, and a number of small hamlets that also needed to be avoided.

I remembered in one of the early flight briefings by John Gore when he explained that the dip tube inside the propane tanks did not go straight to the bottom. They bent over, in the direction of the valve, for the last 3 inches in order to avoid picking up any gunk at the bottom of the cylinder. He told me if I ever ran out of fuel you could undo the strap holding the propane tank and tip it over at 45 degrees to get another two or three burns out of the tank. I did just that and approached the field which I had selected with just 20 per cent of fuel left in the entire bal-loon. I was lucky to find an ideal field and came in steep with no abort options. We landed perfectly safely and we had both learned a valuable lesson.

Chapter Eleven

Africa Calling

It was apparent from my earlier trip to Kenya that the balloon experience over the Serengeti was spectacular but very seasonal and would not provide enough passengers all of the year round. The optimum time to fly in a balloon was during the migration season when the great herds of wildebeest followed the grass north in their millions. It was always nice to float over the Serengeti, with its vast areas of grasslands and bush, interesting flora and fauna, rolling hills, valleys to explore and pockets of game to observe and fly amongst, but I was looking for more than that.

I travelled to Dar es Salaam, the capital city of Tanzania, and talked to various ministers and civic officials before moving on to the city and erstwhile capital of Arusha. It is a very traditional African city, full of market traders and street vendors where you could buy a coconut which would be expertly 'dressed' with a sharp machete, the top removed to provide a cooling drink of the healthy nectar within. Once emptied of coconut milk the vendor would take to the machete again to chop up the moist chunks of flesh to sustain you on your journey.

I decided to take a long drive of more than 120 miles to journey west of the city, to the unique Ngorongoro. The main feature is the Ngorongoro Crater, the world's largest inactive, intact and unfilled volcanic caldera. The crater, which formed when a large volcano exploded and collapsed on itself two to three million years ago, is 2,000 feet deep and its floor covers 100 square miles.

The term 'unique' is often misused but Ngorongoro is truly that. There is not another un-flooded crater on the planet of such magnitude and it provides a safe haven for many species of animals including the big five – lion, African elephant, Cape buffalo, leopard and rhinoceros. My guide, Paul, was an ex-ranger and knew the area intimately, taking me to places untrodden by the white man. We entered Masai villages nestling around the sun-baked rim of the crater, who fed us on village maize, traditionally ground by the women folk, and freshly slaughtered goat, cooked with onions and local vegetables over charcoal fires and eaten beside a bonfire outside the chief's house. While feasting on this wholesome fare we were entertained by the females dancing and the Masai warriors performing their traditional ceremonial jumping. They were all dressed in the most colourful of tribal clothes, accompanied by African chanting and drumming, producing a cacophony of harmoni-ous music and colour that only the Africans can create. The evenings were drawn to a close with the men drinking village brewed beer which was disgusting, but preferable to the cows' blood drank by some. I sipped quietly on my bottled water, enthralled by the magic and splendour of it all.

If we decided to bring hot air balloons to this location, we would need a lodge at which to base the balloons, which would hopefully be populated by tourists of the adventurist type who would like to experi-ence a new adventure and an opportunity to view the bush, villages and the inhabiting game from the baskets of my balloons. We drove off the main track on a red dirt road to a lodge that Paul explained was the best appointed in the area. As we rounded a corner in the track the lodge revealed itself, nestling in a slight hollow below. It was a picture book setting that personified most people's view of what the African bush should be. A cluster of small grass topped round houses surrounded a huge circular building at the centre of this 'village' with a watering hole on the west side of the encampment that completed the scene, with small and elevated viewing platforms overlooking another large water-ing hole. I could picture my tourists sitting there, attired in safari suits while drinking iced gin and tonics as the huge African sun slipped slowly behind the water on a cool evening. As we approached the entrance to the lodge there were four giraffes, ambling slowly along, feeding on the succulent leaves at the tree tops while a small group of zebra grazed on the natural pastures that surrounded the facility and several types of buck stood, twitching nervously, among the herd as we drove past. Even Paul, an African bush veteran, commented on the beauty of it all and I thought I had found the most perfect tourist heaven on the globe. But this was the bush and things were not always as they first seemed.

We were escorted around the village and shown our quarters. The small round house rooms were adequate and clean, each with its own bathroom. I decided to shower before dinner but there did not seem to be any running water. Over the shower tray there was a large leather bag with a chrome shower head attached underneath. The lodge manager explained that when I needed a shower I was to tell the room boy who would heat a bucket of water and pour it into the bag ready for me to open the shower head while positioned beneath it. The same procedure was in place for the toilet. Once used, the room boy could be summoned to tip a bucket of water down the loo to flush it. There was electricity provided by a generator and during the hours of darkness we were asked to switch the lights on and off several times which would indicate to the room boy that they were needed. I wondered how the more discerning female visitors would react to this procedure and was told that they did not have many lady visitors, the guests were almost always men. The warming of the water took thirty minutes, but it worked well and I looked forward to dinner, a cool beer and some pleasant conversation later on at the viewing platform, overlooking the watering hole where the game came to drink.

We walked over to the dining room, which was simply furnished in traditional rustic African style, and the manager took us on a tour of the kitchen. It was a very large block, with state of the art appliances and fittings. The manager proudly pointed out each piece of equipment, Zanussi fridges and freezers, ovens and hobs manufactured in Europe, ice makers imported from America and the latest blenders, electric toasters and espresso coffee machines that would enhance even the finest of western kitchens. The problem was that not one single piece of the equipment was being used.

The alleged chef, a chap from a nearby village dressed in blue motor mechanic overalls, was cooking in the middle of the kitchen using charcoal on an upturned, cut in half oil drum. They had hacked out a hole in the roof of the kitchen to take out the smoke. I asked him what he was cooking and he simply said, 'Food, I am cooking food.'

It turned out to be goat and onions again but this time with chips, which had been cooked in oil that was not hot enough and rendered them inedible. The local bread, baked outside in a brick oven, turned out to be surprisingly good. Dessert was an apple. I was offered a cold beer which I accepted unenthusiastically as I knew what was coming. In these parts the definition of cold means 'It's not hot', the only beer cooling system being a bucket of well water which reduces the temperature to just below tepid.

Given that the food and accommodation could be adequately referred to as basic, I asked how many visitors attended each year.

'Very few people come and they don't come for the food but for the animals,' boasted Paul, adding, 'Here we have the best animals in all Africa. It is God's country.'

I remarked that there seemed to be no tariff for the accommodation and he explained that it was all inclusive as the visitors paid big money to hunt the animals. This resort was built to pander for the type of visitor that would pay a great deal to shoot the animals. They would be picked up on arrival at Dar es Salaam International airport, go straight to the lodge, staying one night, rise early to be escorted to a selected target which had been already identified by the trackers. They would shoot the animal, have a photograph taken with the 'kill' and take the next airplane out having paid a staggering fee. The 'hunters' collect trophies which are scored on the basis of certain measurements, lengths of tusks for elephants, horn for rhinos, head for lions etc. It was a sickening system, and some of the animals were even drugged to make it easier for the so-called hunter. It was total exploitation and a ruthless slaying of some of the most beautiful animals in the world.

The following morning we were exploring the bush and I felt a compulsion to debate the question and the morality of big game hunting with Paul. It was obvious that the lodge saw very few visitors indeed and was there to simply pander to a section of people that could afford to make a hobby out of killing the animals for fun. It would enable them to take home a trophy, normally the head of the beast, allowing them to play out the 'Great White Hunter' act to their friends and contemporaries, presumably boasting about the adventure and excitement of it all. It was neither of those. Paul argued that it was a good thing as it brought money to the area. Hunters would pay between $30,000 and $50,000 for a single shot. He felt that as there were a great many animals in the area, big game hunting had no long term effect or damage on the animal welfare and population, from a conservation view point anyway. My views had little effect on Paul; he simply could not understand the passion of my argument against this abhorrent blood sport.

A day later we passed a kill in the bush, but this was neither nature taking its course or the result of a trophy hunter. It was the kill of a poaching team and the victim was a rhinoceros with its horn hacked off. It was very recently dead as the other animals had only just started to devour the carcase.

It was a very sad and disturbing sight and, exasperated, I asked, 'Why do they do it, Paul?'

'Money, Mr Mike, money,' he replied.

'But money is what you accept for allowing the hunters to kill game, what's the difference?' I asked with concern. Another discussion took place on the moralities and financial rewards of this type of profit hunting and there was some sort of moral dilemma emerging. It was clear that they all respected and loved the African animals and were fiercely protective of them in so many ways, the upkeep of the habitat, the protection from close-up human intrusions and the absolute hatred for the poacher. There was also a fierce determination to catch them.

Paul described to me the two types of poaching that they dealt with. Firstly, there was the local poacher who only hunted for food. They were supposed to treat all classes of poachers in the same way, by arresting them and taking them to Arusha to place them in jail ready for criminal trial. Paul explained that they did not bother with this. Local poachers were simply beaten up.

'They are poor people,' Paul said, 'and only do it to feed themselves and their families.'

I asked about the professional poachers, did they take them to jail? He told me that these teams carried guns and it was a lot of effort to travel to Arusha so they were often 'dispatched' in the bush. It was, he explained, 'proper justice' and the poachers' bodies were left to feed the animal they were trying to kill. It was 'God's way'.

Taking a last glimpse at the sad carcase, I have to say that I was an agnostic on this argument after witnessing this horror.

I left the area to catch an airplane, from Arusha back to Dar es Salaam on the Tanzanian National Airline which was run by the Russians. The check-in staff were mostly made up of locals but the managers and air-craft crews were Russian citizens, dressed in the traditional military style uniform with the large rim caps and smart brass buttoned uniforms. It all looked a little odd in Africa.

I was a little surprised that the terminal was so empty and Paul's driver Joseph, who was escorting me to the aircraft, kept saying, 'Mr Mike, the aircraft has gone.'

I knew this could not be the case as I was an hour early, as clearly instructed for domestic flights, but I was beaten again by the African system.

The check-in girl took my ticket, studied it for a few seconds and gave it me back. 'The aircraft has left,' she said.

'But I have a ticket and the flight was not scheduled to leave for another hour,' I remonstrated.

'Everybody arrived here for the flight so they let it go early,' she responded.

'Everybody was not here,' I said, shaking my ticket at her. 'I wasn't here!'

'But there were other people here who wanted your seat,' she answered, adding 'you can come back tomorrow.'

Losing your temper just does not work in these parts and I could see that complaining to the Russian managers was futile judging from the 10 or so other passengers lined up in front of the manager's desk. The official, a plump Russian, sat behind the desk, not even recognising the presence of the people queuing up in front of him. There was no choice but to ask Joseph to drive me to the town to find a hotel for the night. We drove back towards the town and were stopped, almost immediately, by a road block. It was in the form of a railway sleeper, pulled across the narrow road and was fitted with large spikes protruding out of the top edge.

We were instantly surrounded by five or six armed men in scruffy uniforms and wearing berets. They ordered us out of the car and began barking questions at me. Joseph was answering them in the local language in a furious and agitated exchange. One of the men took me aside as the argument continued and asked if I had any money. It was very dark and I felt vulnerable but I was called back to Joseph and the obvious leader of this group.

Joseph explained, 'The boss man said we have to go with this man,' indicating to another quasi-soldier with a rifle. They put me in the back seat and the man got in the front with Joseph driving. As we drove off I asked Joseph, who was visibly sweating at the wheel, 'Where are we going?' He told me he did not know but the man was giving him directions. We went on to an isolated dirt road and followed the direction in which he pointed. I had no idea where we were headed or what was going to happen to us. I noticed that the weapon on the man's left side between his shoulder and the seat was an old Enfield 303 rifle – not exactly current army issue but any weapon in civilian hands was a valuable and dangerous possession. I had an idea. I told Joseph that when I shouted 'STOP' he was to hit the brakes as hard as possible. As we approached a crossroads on the dirt track I shouted the instruction and Joseph slammed the brakes on. The passenger pitched into the dash board and I pulled the rifle out. As the man turned around to see what was happening I threw the rifle out of the back window and into the dark night. It worked, he opened the passenger door and leaped out to attempt to recover his prized possession.

I shouted, 'DRIVE, DRIVE, DRIVE!' Joseph started to drive, wide-eyed and astonished, and then stopped abruptly. 'GO, GO!' I screamed and Joseph drove off very quickly, not slowing down until we felt out of range of the possibility of a bullet coming through the rear window.

I asked him who these people were and he told me they were not policemen or the army and that they were not bandits.

'They are just men with guns, Mr Mike, and I told them that I worked for Mr Paul and they let us go, no problem.' I asked if he knew where the man was taking us and he said he did not know and was just following the man's directions but added that he may have been using us to take the man with the gun home! If that was the case it was a terrifying way to get a lift. Well, all things considered, I thought, as we drove to a hotel, I wonder what I could have done to make myself feel like an even bigger dickhead.

The journey to Dar es Salaam went to plan the next day and I stayed with a family of Indian friends, relishing the home cooked curries and desserts that were prepared and served by my friend Akbar's first wife. He had another in Nairobi that had looked after me in a similar fashion on several other occasions.

Dar es Salam had a cosmopolitan population with a huge Asian community, the food markets were full of oriental spices and fresh fruits and I have to admit that the indigenous people included some of the most spectacular girls I have ever seen. Nevertheless, it was apparent that Tanzania was not ready for a large influx of tourists that could support my balloon passenger endeavours. I would have to look somewhere else.

It came to me in a flash - what about Egypt? I imagined flying over the great Pharaonic Monuments, the Pyramids of Giza and the rolling sand dunes of the Sahara desert flanking the fertile regions of the Nile Delta. And, very importantly, many thousands of tourists. Yes, I would go there.

I had won a contract for a Midlands-based ice-cream maker and I proposed that we build a special shape balloon replicating a giant ice-cream cornet. A part of the presentation to the clients proposed that we built the balloon at the Royal Show, Stoneleigh, Warwickshire, and fly it out of the show to great publicity. The client went for it and Dick Wirth, the MD of Thunder Balloons, agreed to hire an exhibition unit and bring in machines and seamstresses to build the balloon. It was a fabulous success and I registered the balloon as G-ICES. It took off, to plan, from the show and we spent the summer attending large public events and flying major customers for the ice-cream maker; Ashford.

However for my next trip I was off to Germany. We had won a lucrative promotional contract for the Royal Mail. A big red balloon with the royal crest was commissioned and built which we flew at major Royal Shows around the country, promoting the postal service. Captain Jim Howard of the 14th/20th King's Hussars, based in Germany, had persuaded the regiment to build its own balloon. The Guidon Parade was being scheduled, the presentation of new colours for the regiment and I was asked if I would attend the ceremony with the Royal Mail balloon and fly it, in a competition alongside a small group of selected pilots and balloons in front of the regiment's commander, Her Royal Highness Princess Anne.

The regimental barracks were quite close to Belsen, the site of one of the infamous Nazi concentration and death camps. We visited the site and this made a lasting and profound impression on me. The platform of the railway station had been built in huge proportions just to handle the great volume of human traffic that was delivered to the camp. It was unnerving to realise the extent of the methodical planning and infrastructure that was resourced to assure a smooth and efficient procedure in the business of mass murder.

The Belsen camp is a solemn place and I felt the atmosphere immediately as I stepped through the entrance gate. It was as though someone had stolen the oxygen out of the place as I gulped for breath inside the main compound. The enormity of this cruel period of history penetrated my inner consciousness and stuck there like a foreign body lodged deep inside of me. The several massive mounds of earth each indicating the graves for several thousand victims stood as terrible monuments in an unnatural silence. There were no birds singing or flying over the area and the stillness was palpable. As I walked out, a family of three, approaching the gate, collapsed on the ground in sobbing distress as they entered the complex and I wondered what emotions, depths of helpless despair and horrors they were about to encounter as they sought some kind of solace or comfort, or answers, in this place of death and heartbreaking memories. Everyone should go there.

The balloons were laid out in a field outside the barracks with the baskets on the side and inflation fans at the ready. The pilots and crew were all waiting in anticipation as Princess Anne came along to talk to the balloonists. Her visit to my balloon was prearranged, well, it was the Royal Mail after all and the Commander in Chief stopped at my side to discuss the impending inflation and flight. HRH was most keen to hear all about the balloon and I explained the equipment and how it operated. She seemed enthralled with the theory of lighter than air flight and I explained the sensation in as glowing terms as possible, to which she responded with interest and enthusiasm. 'It all sounds terribly exciting,' she remarked, 'and a real adventure.'

'It is, Ma'am,' I said and cheekily added, 'I would be happy to fly you, this will be a hare and hounds competition and the 14th/20th King's Hussars balloon is the hare. As a hound, I will follow – so you will be in good company.'

She explained that she was not allowed in a balloon and I informed her that I understood that. In fact, no member of the Royal Family had ever flown in a hot air balloon but I assured HRH it was quite safe.

Captain James Howard interjected, glowering at me for raising the subject, a point that I had been specifically briefed on, but Princess Anne was obviously interested, asking how long the flight was, where we would land, what height would the balloon go to and when would we get back. I thought I had almost convinced her when she was ushered away and was asking me when we would take off.

'Exactly thirty minutes, Ma'am,' I said, as she walked away.

The balloon was inflated and the hare balloon had already taken off. I had waited a little over thirty minutes and was ready for lift-off. As I rose out of the field the Princess, having changed into jeans and sweater, came running over, waving her arms. It was too late, my balloon was hot and rising. I was out of there but she shouted, 'Come back to the mess and tell us how you got on!'

The flight went very well but we got very close to the so-called Berlin Wall that separated the country, with sentry boxes every few yards. We landed in a muddy potato field and were caked in mud by the time we had carried the balloon out and driven back to the barracks.

My crew and I presented ourselves at the mess with all of the military personnel in splendid full dress uniforms, while we, in contrast, were in wellington boots and mud encrusted red flying suits. A smart lieutenant politely informed us that we could not come in, explaining that it was a black tie evening. I said that the Commander in Chief had invited us to come to the mess after the balloon flight. He asked if we would mind awfully if we waited for a moment, while he checked, and left us in order to confer with his superior officer. While he was away we changed our wellingtons for shoes that were in the retrieve vehicle, took off the flying suits and replaced them with the Royal Mail flying jackets. It was hardly full dress but a lot more respectable. The lieutenant returned with his captain, said we were most welcome and directed us through the mess and into a grand marquee where the regimental band was in full swing. The Princess was in attendance looking very beautiful in a stunning off-white evening dress. We drank and ate throughout the night with the Princess eager to hear all of the details of the flight, from take off to landing. She came and sat at our table and we were still chatting when we took breakfast at 4.30am – a feast of wild rice and prawns, with soft fresh German breads and strong German coffee.

I had done well in the competition and should have won a prize, at least, and the presentations were due to be awarded at the Survivors Supper, the traditional name for a party at the conclusion of all balloon meets. At the end of the presentations, from which I was ominously missing, Captain Howard announced that the attendees may be surprised at the omission of one particular pilot.

'Mike Kendrick has been disqualified from the competition for hogging the attention of the Princess.' It was very funny and I was called to the rostrum to be presented with a plaque to commemorate this occasion. I treasure it more than the many winning silver and pewter cups and mugs that sit in my study.

Hang-gliders and Microlights were starting to emerge by the late 1970s and early 1980s and I began to evaluate them to determine the potential of commercial applications. The hang-glider was basically a V-shaped wing which the flyer attached to themselves and then jumped off hills. We had dropped some hang-gliders from balloons at various heights but these applications were very limited. The powered hang-glider then emerged which offered a pilot and passenger capability and was a very inexpensive method of flying for enthusiasts wanting to get their feet off the ground. Hang-gliders were flown by a basic weight shift method – the pilot shifting his position, in flight, and pulling at an A-frame to present the wing at different angles in order to manoeuvre. I did fly one of these machines around the sky for an hour or two but found it a little boring and could not see any long term sponsorship potential.

Microlights were a little different. They were basically a lightweight, fabric-covered aircraft with three access controls. In other words, they were flown like a normal light aircraft, with elevators and rudders and some could carry two people. I went to a major air show called Oshkosh in Wisconsin, USA, to see them flown and was impressed by this American development. There was a group of pilots in the UK that were keen on flying these machines and they did have a display capability at events and air shows so I bought two of them and funded a new start-up company run by one of the pilots.

At the same time a new type of hot air balloon was also being designed called 'Cloudhoppers'. It was the brain child of Colin Prescott, my leading competitor in the hot air balloon business. The cloudhopper was a very small balloon without a basket. The pilot was strapped into a harness with the burner and fuel tank at the back. The pilot hung below the balloon from the harness with a burner handle available at his right hand. The flight time was very limited as there was only enough fuel for around thirty minutes and a beeping noise would tell you when the fuel was low. The harness had a quick release mechanism so that the pilot could release rapidly on touching the ground. Cloudhoppers were great fun and exciting to fly. The 'Airchair' was also being built which similarly did not have a basket and comprised of a purpose-made seat, underneath which contained two cylinders for extra duration and could fly a pilot and passenger.

I used the Airchair and Microlights for a film called 'The Alpine Challenge', which was set in St Moritz in Switzerland. It was a James Bond spoof based on a series of TV commercials with the tag line, 'All because the lady loves Milk Tray.' The goodie was trying to deliver a box of chocolates to a lady and the baddies were trying to stop him. The hero would be chased by villains on skis down the mountain and would climb into my balloon, fully inflated and ready to fly, to escape. Once the balloon was in the air the villains would come out of the sky in the Microlights, fitted with rockets and shoot the balloon down and this chase went on and on until he delivered the chocolates to the beautiful lady waiting patiently in her boudoir. I wanted to test out the Airchair I had with me to see how high it would get, just for fun. There were several ballooning sequences to be filmed but before those started I took the Airchair to a plateaux on the mountain. I fixed an inflation fan to the chair and experimented with using the fan as an engine to propel the balloon. The idea was to use the rotation vents to spin the balloon around, so that the fan was always at the rear, thereby achieving a steerable balloon.

It was not such a good idea. The balloon ascended, fan running, me steering, climbing slowly making a forward speed on about 4 knots, albeit at an odd angle produced from the push from the fan. I was quickly satisfied that the plan was never going to work properly when I became aware of a dripping noise on my crash helmet and looking up saw that the balloon fabric was melting and a large hole was appearing at the top. Oh dear, I thought, the balloon could not sustain the extra weight of the inflation fan strapped onto it and I was on the way down. I was thankful that thick snow facilitated a nice soft landing.

This trip also gave me the opportunity to ski for the first time. I had a couple of lessons on the nursery slope and then went up to the top of the mountain and launched myself off. Young, enthusiastic and over-confident, I skied down, going very fast, until I came to a banked corner. I could see the top half of a chalet behind the bank and was unable to negotiate the left hand turn. I went straight over the bank, ended up on the patio of a chalet and stopped abruptly at the French window, looking into the lounge. There were three people there, drinking the local Gluvine – a delicious hot mulled red wine. The inhabitants rose off their chairs, opened the French window and ushered me through the room to the opposite window, not uttering a word throughout the entire process, and let me out of the that window, with me muttering a rather embarrassed 'thank you,' as I re-joined the piste. Obviously, this was not a unique occasion for them.

But we had a movie to make and I had no more leisure time left before the next film sequences were shot – which were to land me injured in a Swiss hospital.

The most difficult sequence to shoot involved the hero skiing down towards my waiting balloon, ready for take off on a frozen lake. He would ski down the hill followed by two villains, come to a stop at the basket, hop in and I would take off with him on board – thereby escaping the foul intentions of those trying to catch him. We waited, with the balloon standing up fully inflated on the ice. It was a long wait as the hero tried to ski down the slope but he kept falling over and we were on the sixth take before he managed to scramble into the basket. We took off and rose to several thousand feet when the hero leaped out and skydived away, chased by the villains who had jumped out of a helicopter. More villains, in Microlights would attack the balloon with rockets. It would all be cut together in the editing room, along with the balloon crash footage, next to be filmed.

The balloon crash scene was simple enough. I was to fly to 500 feet above a frozen lake, with a cameraman on board. Microlights, flown by more bad guys, would come out of the clouds firing rockets at the balloon to shoot me down. I would deflate the balloon and crash on to the ice. I briefed the cameraman very carefully, making sure he understood that he would have to stop filming before the impact. I was concerned that if he had the viewing lens on his eye at the moment of impact it would cause a very nasty injury. I drilled this into him several times.

I levelled out at 500 feet and watched the Microlight pilots, Richard and Barry, attacking the balloon in a brilliant exhibition of stunt flying. The director, filming all this from the lake, gave me the 'NOW' instruction over the radio and I pulled the rip line opening the parachute rip, deflating the balloon. The balloon envelope distorted immediately and we screamed towards earth as if we had been shot down.

I quickly shouted to the cameraman to hold the basket ropes and stay in the basket but he was concentrating on 'getting the shot', oblivious to my instructions. Just before we impacted he still had the camera to his eye and I was forced to grab the camera away from his eyeball as we hit the frozen lake. This meant I was out of the landing position and on impact my elbows hit the fuel cylinders, very hard, and I knew instantly that my shoulders were either broken or dislocated. I was unable to move my arms to fully deflate the balloon so it rose into the air again. I shouted at the cameraman to pull the rip line and we eventually came down with another hard smack.

I was taken to hospital, in great pain, but the medical professionals in that area are hugely experienced in injury and trauma and sorted me out very quickly. They sat me on a bed and injected the left shoulder. As the needle went in I felt it hit the bone and the doctor said, 'Does this hurt?'

'It's OK,' I said.

He looked at me and replied, 'Now it will hurt,' as he emptied the contents of the syringe into the affected area. After repeating the process with the right shoulder, some manipulation was carried out and I have to say I was out of pain and released from the hospital within thirty minutes.

I was anxious to get back to the lake and check how it all went from the film director's point of view and was relieved to hear from him that he felt it was great footage and I congratulated the Microlight pilots for their flying. Barry was still full of adrenaline and was looking forward to the party now being organised for that evening. Barry was a fine aviator and lived for flying.

Unfortunately I was to watch him die in front of me a few weeks later.

Chapter Twelve

Technology, Tragedy and Tutankhamun

Per Lindstrand approached me with a vision. He had an idea of breaking the world altitude record standing at 56,000 feet currently held by British balloonist Julian Knott. Per had an adventurous plan that he thought would enable a balloon with two pilots to get above 80,000 feet – to the edge of space. I remember thinking, 'Shit – 80,000 feet – and I don't like heights.' But I agreed to meet him to discuss the feasibility of such a project. It was going to be a dangerous undertaking and I now had a new baby to consider. My wife's pregnancy had been difficult and she had miscarried two years before so I did not want to worry her with such a madcap project at this point. She was taken into hospital as the baby was breeched and I got a call at two o'clock in the morning to tell me the baby was on the way and was being delivered by caesarean section. I jumped in the car and immediately realised I needed to tell my friend Robert Jones. Rob had supported me at both of the boy's births. They were born at home and I was a nervous wreck, on both occasions. Rob had sat with me through the process and I thought he would want to know what was happening. I stopped at a phone box on the way to Wolverhampton and called him to tell him I was on the way to the hospital.

'OK,' he said, 'pick me up on the way.'

I did and we arrived at the hospital thirty minutes later. The baby hadn't waited for us; we walked straight through to the delivery room as Anne was being wheeled out with our new baby son.

The startled staff looked at us and said, 'Who's the father?' a question we answered by Rob and I both raising our hands simultaneously. And then fell about laughing. So our third son had to be named Robert.

Two weeks later I was in the hangar at our base in Halfpenny Green airport, thinking about this new baby and the miracle of it all, and I was reminded how precious and fickle life really was when Barry, flying a Microlight with a student pilot, was killed. It was a very warm day with strong thermal activity, making it very unstable, certainly not balloon flying weather and I had watched the enthusiastic flyer take off from the grass strip with his passenger and observed the aircraft circle around the field. I was standing in the hangar when I felt a rush of cold air, indicating that a thermal had risen rapidly. The force of this rising column of hot air took the Microlight out of the sky and dumped it into an adjoining field instantly killing Barry and his passenger. It was horrifying. These two young people enjoying themselves, flying for fun, not expecting to be tested this day by the uncertainties of flight and the risks involved. I did what I could to help the families under these terrible circumstances but, in reality, you can do nothing substantial to ease the pain of losing a loved one. Nothing.

Meanwhile, new contracts were coming in, we had a large stable of balloons, including the recent addition of a special shape bottle of whiskey for White Horse and a travel insurance company, called Mondial, had commissioned two balloons, a 77 (three people) and a cloudhopper, the small balloon with a back pack that was useful in confined areas, including inside shopping precincts. We often flew the two balloons together with the cloudhopper pilots hanging on to the big balloon's crown line as it rose out of a showground in close formation, to the delight of the watching crowds.

Per and I met and he explained his theory involved in the establishment of a new and unbeatable altitude record. The problems with very high altitude flights were many and varied requiring new thinking and new technology. Firstly, it was necessary to keep the burner alight which was very difficult above 50,000 feet, as the oxygen level would be low and a burner could not function without an adequate supply. Secondly, it would need to be flown with the pilots in full spacesuits or in a pressurised capsule. Neither had been done before. Per's idea was to build a balloon with a bullet-shaped envelope, rather than the conventional inverted tear drop shape, which was capable of climbing at over 4,000 feet per minute. The theory was that, when the burner stopped functioning due to lack of oxygen, the momentum of the balloon would carry it up to an estimated 80,000 feet before it began its inevitable descent back to earth.

80,000 feet is an altitude within the last two per cent of the remaining atmosphere, where the curvature of the earth would be clearly visible at the 'edge of space'. The initial plan was to take off in the UK and splash down in the English Channel in a NASA/Apollo type scenario, when divers would jump from chase helicopters to retrieve the crew. A sea touchdown called for a pressurised capsule, rather than spacesuits in an open gondola. Spacesuits were not really an option since we had to be able to evacuate the gondola quickly and parachute to safety in an emergency. Spacesuits and parachutes don't go well together, they restrict movement and it would be difficult to evacuate the capsule quickly and pull a parachute rip cord. At these great altitudes split second lifesaving decisions may have to be made. It was to be an exciting and risky endeavour and I knew I should not do it, but I also knew I would be forever twisted with regret if I did not take on this enormous and seemingly impossible challenge. It was also a high tech project combining ballooning and space technology and would involve the assistance of leading technology experts, risk assessment consultants, the military, UK search and rescue agencies and would also require a management team to handle such a large and complex project. It would also cost a great deal of money. Where would I get that from?

While I contemplated the feasibility of this project and juggled with the risks involved, I was still determined to make ballooning available to the public and made contact with a credible businessman in Cairo. I arranged to meet Ahmad El Sawy and boarded an EgyptAir flight to this great city, home to 18 million people. I was driven from the airport through the suburb of Heliopolis and past the huge and historic temple of the prophet Muhammad and onto the Nile island of Zamalek, the location of my hotel. I have been in many large cities but Cairo has a personality all of its own, where the contrast of wealth and destitution, education and illiteracy sit and coexist together in quiet recognition of the huge difference between the rich and the poor. While unrest lingered beneath the surface, with a despotic dictator-led government, I detected a two-way respect between the occupants of the high end villas that sat alongside the slums and hovels inhabited by the poor.

My task was to investigate the potential of creating a spectacular, safe and unforgettable balloon flight experience. The first and obvious point of call was The Great Pyramid of Giza, in close proximity to the Nile, a juxtaposition of the wonderful, desert based Pharaonic Dynasties, over thousands of years and the hustle and bustle of the fertile shores of the iconic river with its myriad of sail powered feluccas and crowded souks alongside modern day cottage industries.

I was driven towards the pyramids along the 'Green Pyramid' road, named for its topiary, fashioned into pyramid shapes for its entire length. Elegant villas of outstanding quality lined each side, punctuated by new buildings constructed on the sites of demolished villas and I wondered how this was allowed by the planning authorities. I was told that it was not allowed, but the policy of the government was to impose a fine on the developers that equalled the entire cost of any new building. The effect of this was a tacit approval to allow it to happen, the government collected revenues in fines while the developers simply added the fine costs on to the sale price. The only loser was Cairo, with this element of its heritage gone forever.

The journey to the pyramids was good, which meant that the tourist transit time from downtown Cairo would be reasonable. A balloon flight meant an early pre-dawn start, without the added burden of a long commute to a launch site. I approached the pyramids with an air of wonder, passing the Sphinx sitting in a splendidly protective pose at the entrance to Giza. The Sphinx is a resplendent creature and I was reminded of its more recent treatment when Napoleon Bonaparte used it as target practice for his cannons. The cannon shot blew off the nose of the Sphinx, which now resides in the British Museum. I have always wondered why we have not given it back to be reinstalled in its rightful place.

The area around the pyramids is mostly open desert, three large pyramids dominating the scene with other burial chambers, for lesser royals, dotting the area. It looked perfect, offering the most spectacular views from a balloon basket and I climbed up the Great Pyramid, also known as the Pyramid of Cheops, to give me an idea of the potential of the aerial view. To the south I could see, far in the distance, other pyramids, including the stepped and crooked pyramids that were an earlier attempt to get the design right. The desert area needed to be surveyed and I had come dressed and prepared for that. I needed to hire a horse and there were plenty available. The options were horse or camel, I knew which option I preferred and quite looked forward to a gallop across the dunes. The only problem I faced was that I wanted an unescorted ride and negotiated with the horse stable owner, oddly named George. He desperately argued to accompany me but I wanted to go alone and meander around wherever I pleased. I had a map of the area and did not want the hassle of taking George with me. Normally, the horses were rented out in groups for one-hour periods, escorted by George or his assistants, but we haggled over the cost and I paid for two hours. George selected a chestnut mare of around 15 hands. I mounted the horse, adjusted the stirrups and trotted out of the stable block to explore the area, two bottles of mineral water stowed in the saddle bag.

I had undertaken some weather research and was aware that the predominant winds had an easterly component, so I was interested to explore the probable landing areas to the west and south of Giza. I looked at the map and was keen to get to a ridge, to the south of the pyramids, which would afford me a panoramic view. However, it became clear that the mare had already decided on which route she wanted to take. We went at a walk to the foot of the great pyramid and I gave the mare the aid to turn left, to which she responded, going into an unasked fast trot. We got clear of the pyramids and headed south, in the general direction that I wished to survey, but then she turned east and would not get back on track south, despite my protestations. She went back into a walk, refusing to stop or turn left and then suddenly went straight from walk into canter, heading in an entirely different direction, and then into a full gallop. I have to say it was exhilarating but she was not answering to my aids and I thought 'you cow!' but decided to let her have her head. They say that 'if rape is inevitable, lie down and enjoy it,' so I did. The mare was in charge and I leant forward in the saddle, grabbed a handful of mane to secure myself, shouted 'goo on!' and we went at full tilt across the desert sands. The mare was magnificent and at full gallop, negotiating every obstacle, nook and cranny that carried a hint of danger over this terrain that she knew so well. She came to a controlled stop after what felt like many adrenalin fuelled furlongs, giving us both time to get our breath back and pause to take in the landscape. She had positioned herself to give a perfect view of the entire area, which I reasoned she did several times each week for the tourists. Of course, I still needed to explore the areas that I had set out to do and I hoped that now that she had had her way with me, she would be more responsive to the bit and do as I asked. She waited for exactly ten minutes before she let me know she was ready to move on and I attempted to steer her back in the direction I wanted to go. The mare was having none of it and simply took me on a tour around the pyramids, stopping occasionally at points that I presumed were of specific interest to the tourists hungry for historical knowledge and legend. So at the end of the 'tour' she completed the ride by going into another short gallop and trotted back to the stable where George was sitting waiting for us with a smug and knowing look on his face.

He looked at his watch and said, 'You've only been one hour.'

'I know,' I said, adding in a feeble attempt to avoid my embarrassment, 'I have seen enough.' I did ask him for a rebate on the two hour fee but he remonstrated with me, explaining that I had hired the horse for two hours and I could keep her for another hour if I wanted to.

'It's up to you, Mr Mike, keep her for another hour. Enjoy.' I had been taken for a ride, quite literally, but went away with a smile on my face. It had been terrific.

Back in central Cairo, a political problem was manifesting itself. It became apparent that the authorities would not allow balloons to fly over the pyramids. Although my friend Dick Wirth, the MD of Thunder Balloons, had tethered a balloon in front of the great pyramid some time before in a promotion for Pepsi-Cola. I was sure that this was a problem that could be solved in negotiations with the Ministry for Antiquities, but another potential show stopper was rearing its ugly head. The Giza area was in close proximity to a military base and, given the influence of the military regime in Egypt, that was going to be a difficult nut to crack.

Undaunted, I arranged to fly down to Luxor in Upper Egypt, the location of the Valley of the Kings and many other important historical monuments. It was both a centre that tourists flocked to, to experience these wonders, and a river port for the many Nile cruise boats that transited between Cairo and Aswan - the southern most city lying on the edge of Lake Nasser.

There were two ways to get to Luxor from Cairo. An EgyptAir service was available but seats at short notice were difficult to obtain and our potential partner Ahmad El Sawy was reluctant to travel by the alternative, an overnight train. He explained that the train experience was not good, that it was like travelling by train, boat and airplane, all in one.

I asked him what he meant and he said, 'It's an old train moving on old tracks. You get the noise and discomfort of a slow train. It's like a boat as the train also rocks from side to side.' I asked him where the airplane came into the equation and he added, 'It's like a plane because it is scary and you think you might crash and die at any moment.'

Thankfully, we managed to secure some flight tickets which had the added bonus of me being able to get a bird's eye view of the area as we circled around Luxor Airport before landing.

I was immediately impressed by the ambiance and character of the area as I booked into the Movenpick Hotel situated to the south of Luxor. Reputed to be one of the best hotels in the area, the Movenpick was German owned and built on ground level with the guest accommodation being small round, nicely appointed huts in the garden area of the hotel. I needed someone who knew the area to show me around and was advised by the management to seek out a taxi driver by the name of Mohamed Ezz. I would find Ezz working from the King's Palace, one of the first hotels to be established in the area and located on the Plaza, overlooking the Nile in Luxor. Ezz was not difficult to find, an intelligent, giant of a man born in Luxor, purported to be a *Mr Fix It* who knew everyone.

I needed initial talks with senior management from the Antiquities, Military Commanders, Aviation authorities, Tourist Board officials, Police and Civic dignitaries, but firstly I needed to see if the area was good from a balloon flying point of view. Ezz said he would arrange everything. He was very upfront with me, explaining that he had just come out of prison having run over a young girl in his taxi and killed her. He explained that it was not his fault but in Luxor anyone involved in an accident with a death involved was immediately taken to jail. He had negotiated an arrangement with the victim's father and was now 'Free'. I hired him for three days. It was a relationship that was to last for more than a decade.

The antiquities were spread over a fairly wide area in all directions, offering stunning views to passengers no matter where the wind was coming from. For visitors staying on the east side of the Nile, which is where ninety per cent of the tourist hotels and cruisers were based, a trip to the West Bank was a must see excursion. The Nile was crossed by ferry to Thebes, the City of the Dead, a settlement of traditionally built dwellings with houses colourfully painted with murals depicting their journey to the holy city of Mecca. It was a pilgrimage that the local people would save for over years to enable them to travel there as a mark of their faith and commitment to the devotion and dedication to the prophet Muhammad. Heading north out of Thebes we passed the Colossi of Memnon, the two massive statues of Pharaoh Amenhotep III that have stood in this place for 3,400 years. Then on to the temple of Queen Hatshepsut, a huge and magnificent monument set at the bottom of a sheer cliff face that illuminates the area in a red glow at dawn.

Driving further north we found a cafe, a relic of the area's more recent history, which was the location building for the 1956 Cecil B. DeMille biblical epic, The Ten Commandments. We stopped for coffee and met the aged owner who made a great fuss of Ezz and I. He was keen to show me a black and white photograph mounted in a frame on the cafe wall. It depicted him as young man wearing some of the iconic jewellery discovered when Howard Carter, for whom he then worked, had located and opened the tomb of Tutankhamun in 1923. I made this cafe a regular port of call whenever I was in Luxor, greatly enjoying the company of this gracious old man.

Just around the corner we passed by Carter's house, where he and his team lived while he was looking for the elusive boy king's burial chamber, and then drove into the entrance of the Valley of the Kings. Immediate impressions of this small valley, really a narrow ravine between the cliffs, were disappointing from a pictorial point of view but the unique treasures beneath the surface were mind bogglingly sensational. The beauty of the burial chambers and the engineering and architectural achievements of these ancient dynasties were of unparalleled skill, beyond comprehension and belief. We visited all of the tombs and I talked to Ezz about needing to find a location we could use that would take a balloon over this valley.

He mentioned a place call Wadi Monkey but added, 'It's not a good place, Mr Mike.' Wadi Monkey was located next to the Valley of the Kings. It was perfect. It was large enough to inflate a balloon in and sheltered from the wind by steep cliffs.

'What's wrong with this place?' I asked Ezz and he explained to me that this Wadi was a place of death, where fathers would bring their daughters to kill them when they had shamed the family. When, as he put it, 'They were no more a virgin.'

I told him I understood how these things happened in ancient times, but he quickly interjected to say, 'No, Mr Mike, not ancient times – now, today!' He went on to explain that virginity was very important to the families of Upper Egypt and that the 'stitching up' of young female children was still done to this very day.

It stunned me and I realised that below the surface of the tourist attractions that were immediately and obviously visible, underneath the hard currencies that were flowing into the national economy, lay a people that were largely undisturbed in their cultural and religious beliefs and unchanged in view of what is right and what is wrong. The tenets and traits of a constantly evolving western society would not be unquestioningly absorbed into this predominantly Muslim community, steeped in tradition and ancient history. We may not need to agree with it but we do need to accept it.

The predominant light winds in Upper Egypt came from the north so we explored the area to the south of the Valley of the Kings, past the ancient Ramesseum complex and into the vast stony desert that stretched north all the way to Libya. As I walked around this desert, Ezz stooped down and handed me a clam fossil, indicating that this area was under water in a previous millennium.

In my mind's eye I imagined a flight from Wadi Monkey, high over the Valley of the Kings and the spectacular temple of Hatshepsut. The balloon flight could then proceed further over the Valley of the Queens and the town of Thebes with the green band of vegetation sandwiching the Nile as the balloon drifted slowly south past the Coptic Church to land gently in the desert. On landing a champagne breakfast would be waiting for the passengers, with iced prawns, cereals, cold fruit juices, canapés and fresh coffee and tea. It really was a place where ballooning memories would be made. I had found my perfect location. I left Luxor understanding that the hard work was yet to come. An ambition to work in Egypt was only that and it would take huge amounts of time in planning and negotiation. The protocols, procedures, permits, licensing and bureaucracy were tall mountains that I had to climb and it was two years before I eventually succeeded in achieving that ambition.

The Egyptian authorities had strictly laid down rules and plans for aircraft certifications, pilot qualification, medical requirements, registration procedures, safety and maintenance regulations and training obligations - but absolutely no concept of lighter than air flight. It was not just a question of amending the existing rules, but writing a completely new operating procedure on hot air balloon flight.

The process of obtaining permissions started in the UK with most of the initial work emanating from Ahmad El Sawy in Cairo, which was just as well as my mind had been turned to contemplating the future in terms of the world hot air balloon altitude record challenge.

I had decided to go for it, of course, and my wife Anne, while not entirely enthusiastic, did not forcibly object on the basis that I would probably do it anyway. There was a risk, not only to life but to reputations and the opportunity for embarrassment was clear. I would not countenance failure but had to accept that it was a real factor and may result in catastrophe. However, Per Lindstrand was an erudite, well-educated aeronautical engineer who had eloquently presented analytical reasoning to answer the technical challenges of the project. I appointed Richard Down, who flew a Microlight alongside Barry in St Moritz, to act as Project Co-ordinator and we set about preparing a presentation to sponsors. Almost immediately, interest was shown, surprisingly by the Milk Marketing Board. They had a lot of promotional money in their budget and were currently running a milk promotion with the slogan, 'Milk's Gotta Lotta Bottle', *bottle* being a British slang term for courage. The altitude attempt to the edge of space fitted perfectly into the board's marketing strategy. We drew up detailed budgets for every possible contingency and factored in the potential publicity benefits to the milk brand, the press calls, the TV documentary and the broadcast rights. The Milk Marketing Board approved the £250,000 budget and we prepared to announce the attempt at a press conference in London, calling the project 'Operation Sky Quest' with the slogan, 'To the edge of Space.'

The press pack illustrated the attempt in a step-by-step chronological order, including the building of three balloons, one of them being the attempt balloon itself which was to be the tallest hot air aerostat ever built. Other details included the theory behind the attempt, the training programmes for the crews, which incorporated learning to evacuate the capsule at great heights which would involve a high altitude skydiving course for the pilots (Oh God, I hate heights) and preparing a team of divers for the sea rescue.

The story of the attempt went worldwide and captured the imagination of the British public and press. Offers flooded in with even NASA offering assistance, and we became instantly recognised, overnight. There were constant demands from the media for TV interviews, in depth press and magazine articles and radio shows. These had to be facilitated by the team as they were an important and agreed commitment to the sponsors.

Large sponsored projects such as Operation Sky Quest enter the public domain and nothing is private. The press are always in attendance and if things go well you look a hero. If things go badly you look an idiot.

We were to experience both.

Chapter Thirteen

Operation Sky Quest

The endeavour to reach the edge of space in a hot air balloon seemed to capture the imagination of everyone and NASA offered their help and advice, appointing one of their management team to the project. We were to make many visits to the Johnson Space Centre in Houston, Texas and benefitted greatly from its colossal knowledge of capsule systems, risk assessment, training methods and various special areas of experience.

The immediate concern of the team, including NASA, was the ability of the crew to be able to evacuate the capsule, in an emergency, particularly at high altitude. We would need to be capable of evacuating the balloon capsule at all altitudes. Jumping out at low altitudes was a matter of a simple text book exit through the open door of the capsule. However evacuating the capsule at altitudes above 12,000 feet was a different matter entirely. The operating procedure and flight plan, on ascent, called for the single door of the capsule to be unsealed and open until we reached an altitude of 12,000 feet. Up to that point, in the event of a serious problem we could quickly parachute out through the open door. As the balloon climbed through 12,000 feet the door would be closed and sealed and the capsule pressurised to allow Per and I to operate normally without the need to wear full spacesuits. On the decent the balloon would depressurise at 12,000 feet, releasing the seal and opening the door as we passed through that altitude. Again, this was the procedure in the event that we needed to evacuate the capsule if a problem had occurred and the balloon was descending too rapidly for Per and I to survive the impact with the ground. In the event of a serious failure at any altitude above 12,000 feet we would need to pull a lever to instantly decompress the capsule, in order to open the door and allow us to evacuate. Although we would not be hampered by full-blown spacesuits, we would be wearing pressure suits which hold the vital organs together in the event of the capsule decompressing. When decompression suddenly occurs the suits inflate explosively and it feels like a truck has hit you. We had to learn to cope with that while keeping our wits about us and avoiding disorientation so we could make a safe exit.

At greater heights, with thin oxygen levels, there would not be enough oxygen to breathe while we would be free falling, until we reached an altitude at which we could open the parachutes, so our pressure suits were to be fitted with emergency breathing apparatus. If we jumped out at heights of up to 80,000 feet we would need to switch on this oxygen supply that would keep us breathing until we fell to around 15,000 feet. One of the main problems with free falling from above 50,000 feet was, that in the thin air, we may not be able to stabilise our bodies, sending us into an uncontrollable spin. At a fast spin the blood quickly flows to the body's extremities and the faller may become unconscious. At that point we would have to rely on our parachutes' AOD (Automatic Opening Device) which, if they worked, would open our parachutes, automatically, at 12,000 feet. The chances of surviving an emergency evacuation from those heights were not good.

So, first on the high altitude training agenda was learning how to skydive and keep the body stable in free fall. Per and I flew to Florida with Tom Donnelly, the appointed standby pilot, who was to take the place of either Per or myself should one of us get injured or sick. Also accompanying us was Peter Mason, an experienced Daily Express journalist who had been commissioned to write, 'Operation Sky Quest – The Book'. Peter and I spent a lot of time together throughout the project and he caught the ballooning bug, subsequently becoming a great pilot in his own right.

The NASA team had recommended that we learn an 'accelerated free fall' programme and identified a skydiving centre in Zephyrhills, Florida. The aim was to become proficient at freefall from 14,000 feet. Jumping out of an aircraft at that height provides approximately sixty seconds of free fall time per jump. The traditional way of learning these skills would involve a great deal of time. You would begin with three static line jumps (the parachute opening line attached to the aircraft) from 3,000 feet. You would then progress to a couple of 'dummy rip cord pull' jumps when you would pull the rip cord handle but, just in case you made a mess of it, the static line would be attached anyway. The jumper would then go on to one second delays, pulling his own rip cord, then two second delays and onwards until they were jumping from 12,000 feet and freefalling for a minute. It could take a very long time, particularly with the vagaries of the European weather.

We did not have the luxury of time and arrived in Florida on a Friday evening, with me making my first jump from 14,500 feet on the following Sunday morning. There was no such thing then as tandem jumping, which is popular today and involves you exiting the aircraft attached to an experienced skydiver. The accelerated free fall programme meant you were on your own and learned on the way down.

We were introduced to the team at the jump centre; Jim Hooper (Hoop), his partner Sarah and our two instructors, the wonderfully named Mitch Decoteau and Roland Hilfiker, along with various people who were regular jumpers at the facility. I can honestly say that these people were the most madcap, nutcase, adrenalin junkies I have ever met. They were full-on skydivers, with all that went with that. They loved jumping out of aircraft and partying hard. Very hard. They were also one of the most skilled and dedicated team of professionals I have ever met.

The initial ground training consisted of hanging from a tree in the prone position while they carefully explained the importance of position while falling through the air at 120 miles per hour. They talked through, in great and vivid detail, the effects of getting a leg or arm out of position while falling and trained us on the methods of correcting a spin. Orientation, they explained, was the key. We had to know where we were and what position we were in, every second, checking and adjusting all the way down. The most overriding message, explained Mitch, was to fall face down. As a novice, it was easy to fall with your back facing the ground which could be disastrous as that position may stop the parachute opening properly. The technique of opening the reserve, in the event of a malfunction of the primary parachute, was rehearsed repeatedly until they were satisfied that it was second nature to us.

As we walked to the aircraft for my first jump Mitch reminded me of the most important rule. 'Position,' he said, concluding, 'look down – it's green. Look up – it's blue. If it's not blue, you're falling on your back!'

I recall asking Mitch what the optimum time was to pull the ripcord.

He answered, 'When the people on the ground look like ants,' adding 'if the ants look like people, it's too fuckin' late.'

As the aircraft climbed to altitude, for my first jump, I was as nervous as a kitten. When we reached 14,500 feet Mitch and Roland pointed out the drop zone and surrounding areas to act as landmarks when I was under the canopy. I wanted to vomit.

As rehearsed, we climbed out on to the aircraft step, Mitch on my right, Roland on my left. As instructed, it was up to me to give the command to jump and they would hang on to the sleeves of my jump suit until I pulled the rip cord at 4,000 feet. Somehow I made a good clean exit from the aircraft and hurtled towards the ground with the hugely skilful Mitch and Roland falling at my side. I looked down . . . Yes, it was green and, as instructed, looked at Mitch and Rowland, giving them a signal that all was OK. I checked the altimeter, several times, and expertly Mitch manoeuvred around my body and, as rehearsed, pointed at the rip cord handle. I pulled at 4,000 feet and prayed that the parachute would open, which it did.

We were using specially built large square sports parachutes, rather than the standard Navy conical types. These square parachutes had toggles on each side of the rigging, allowing us to steer, and I grabbed them in my hands and immediately felt I was back in control, my heart rate going back to somewhere near normal as I floated towards the landing field. I immediately oriented myself, thinking how small the landing area was in relation to the miles of swampland surrounding it. That swampland was full of rather unpleasant animals and creepy crawlies that were high on my personal hate list. This included spiders, snakes and, of course, the dreaded alligator. I inched towards the landing field and over the perimeter edge, aiming for the large yellow cross next to the windsock. I approached the cross, upwind, and stalled the parachute, as practiced, about six feet above the ground. If you get this just right you can touch down in the stand up position. I landed on my arse, but that was not too bad for the first attempt.

The days that followed were intense, to say the least, with more training and daily jumps. As we progressed we made jumps alongside a single instructor. We had to master full 360 degree turns to the left, then to the right, backward somersaults, forward rolls and, perhaps the most frightening, putting the body in a 45 degree angle, pointing to the ground and traversing across the sky towards the ground at speeds of up to 180 miles per hour. We were not supposed to skydive through cloud, it broke the regulations, but that was ignored and the white fair weather cumulous were classified, with a nod and a wink as 'industrial haze'. I was surprised to learn that rain drops actually hurt a little as you fell through them and left tiny red marks on your face. Logical when you realise that rain drops are pointed at the top and you are falling on the sharp end.

As we got more proficient the experienced jumpers began having fun with us. I was in the sky on one occasion when a female jumper came into my view and moved towards me, using her hand and body movements as brakes as she got within touching distance. She then moved into my space, grabbed me, gave me a huge hug and kiss and then pushed me away. I immediately went into a series of back spins resulting in blue, green, blue, green, blue, and, to my relief, back to green – land. This prank was referred to by the skydivers as a 'kiss pass' and was sometimes performed naked. My instructor, Mitch, saw all this happening and did what he could to reach me, in case I was in trouble. He later told me that he saw me tumbling and 'had to skydive my ass off to get close to you.' The landing was fine and we all had a great laugh about it while I pretended to have enjoyed it.

We were joined on this trip by a Rory McCarthy who had also enrolled in the accelerated free fall programme. Rory was the consummate aviator and later we worked together when he became a pilot in the Virgin attempt to circumnavigate a hot air balloon around the world. He joined us in the evenings and I played a terrible trick on him and Peter Mason for which I don't think they have ever forgiven me. We had all hit the bar hard, drinking a lot of beer and shots. Peter, in particular, being a Fleet Street hack, knew how to party and drink to excess. We all had a wonderful evening and became terribly drunk. The following morning they made great fun of me when I was on board the jump aircraft and throwing up everywhere. It was unpleasant for them and embarrassing for me as Mitch Decoteau would not let me jump and I had to stay on board the aircraft while Rory jumped out. Rory and Peter ribbed me about it when I returned to the jump zone and openly boasted that they had drunk far more than me and then gone on to another bar after we left, although they could not remember any details at all. This gave me an idea and I briefed the team. We called Rory and Peter and explained that we had received a complaint and that the sheriff was looking for them. I informed them that we were all upset that they had got so drunk and had caused damage to a car. They were mortified and could not remember anything.

I painted the picture saying, 'Apparently, you were both so drunk you came out of the bar and danced on the bonnet of a car, causing $400 in damage.'

The project director, Richard Down, added sternly, 'It's reported the culprits were wearing Sky Quest T-shirts and have damaged the reputation of this project.'

They were truly appalled, embarrassed and ashamed. They knew the potential consequences of the alleged actions, understanding that everything we were doing was being filmed and may appear on British television, having far reaching effects on the project and the British sponsor. We suggested they make a public apology, filmed by the TV crew, just in case we were unable to suppress the news. Peter and Rory agreed and went off to shower in order to appear presentable and smart for this public apology.

They were looking very sad as the cameras started rolling, with hangdog and pained expressions of regret and remorse. It was a long, grovelling, unreserved apology which was obviously sincere and well meant, with offers to pay for the damage to the car. I let them get to the very end, to the watery eye and breaking voice stage, before I told them I had made the whole thing up. They were both incandescent with rage as the whole crew fell about with laughter. They promised me that they would get even very soon.

The jump site owner arrived to pick us up one morning, which was unusual. He was anxious to tell us that there had been an incident at the site. One of the jumpers had a 'deep six', which meant a jumper had hit the ground and been killed after an equipment malfunction. It was a reminder of just how serious this training was. Enjoy yourself but respect what you are doing was the message of the day. A deep six was normally followed by a 'crater party' when friends and fellow skydivers would go and sit around the depression in the ground which was created by the impact. They would sit around the crater drinking Budweiser, reminiscing with stories about the great times and narrow escapes they had all enjoyed together.

Skydiving was an illuminating experience. I was staggered at the ability of the brain to make judgements and decisions at lightning speed. Early on in the training I was briefed to pull the rip cord at 4,000 feet. This was normally lowered in increments of 500 feet as the jumper became more proficient. If you failed to pull, Mitch or Roland would move in and pull the cord. This truly was 'deep end diving' – you really did learn on the way down. I was due to pull at 3,500 feet but the trainers had made a briefing mistake - the only mistake I witnessed them making – and had not been informed that I was pulling 500 feet lower.

I made a good exit and skydived down, looked at my altimeter at 4,000 feet and went back to the free fall position for a moment or two. I then went into the pull position and the rip cord handle was not there. I was immediately in emergency mode and went into reserve chute position, placing my left hand on the reserve handle with my right hand over it. Pulling the reserve chute was a two handed job. I was still falling at 120 miles per hour but my instincts took me back for another look at the main chute handle, which meant going back into free fall position. I did that and rechecked. The rip cord handle was definitely not there and I returned to the reserve pull position. Then I thought, 'If the handle's not there the chute must open,' and at that very moment I felt the main chute opening and descended down to make a perfectly good landing 10 yards from the yellow cross target. It transpired that Roland had not told Mitch that I was pulling at the lower altitude of 3,500 feet and had moved into my side, silently, and seeing I had not pulled the main chute handle, had removed it and flown away. That is how good these guys were.

I found it incredible that my brain had entered into a thought process and made at least three conscious, high energy, decisions and four body manoeuvres in the space of the two or three seconds during which I was plummeting down to earth at 120 miles per hour.

Peter Mason pulled another trick on me the following morning, by disguising his voice and telephoning at six o'clock in the morning to tell me that the jump centre had arranged a special flight for a jump and needed me there in ten minutes sharp. I got there and, of course, the jump site was empty.

That afternoon Peter was talking to his wife in the UK and I got Sarah, Hoop's partner, to pick up the phone extension and shout, 'Peter, I'm out of the shower now!' It caused a hell of a row. Tee hee hee!

The next jump I did was eventful. It had three elements to it and it was frantic, scary and painful. I was getting proficient at skydiving and was jumping alone, without an instructor, although every jump was observed and analysed. A Dakota aircraft was being used by the experienced jumpers and, on this day, it went up with 30 skydivers on board. I was in another aircraft and saw the Dakota jumpers leave the aircraft. I jumped out and we all had fun (as much fun as you can have when terrified) flying around the sky doing back flips. I fell through some rain, experiencing the stinging sensation of hitting the pointy end of the drops again and deployed my parachute. I realised that I was under a black cloud and I did not feel at all safe. I stopped descending and was sucked upwards. The ground disappeared from view as I entered the base of the cloud. The silence was eerie and I was totally disorientated, cocooned in the grey mist with no visibility whatsoever. I knew I had to get out of the grip of this cumulous very quickly. I pulled sharply at the left toggle and spiralled out of the cloud and headed away from that part of the sky as fast as I could, then made a turn towards the drop zone, which now lay dead ahead of me. As I descended I watched the other skydivers going in, literally. A squall had developed, under the cloud from which I had escaped and they were having great difficulty landing. Some of these skydivers had completed more than 3,000 jumps and knew how to handle this situation. I had done 10 jumps and did not have a clue. They all made it without injury and turned to watch me come in, gathering around the yellow cross target, to assist and shout encouragement as I made my approach. I got it just right, with the wind sock pointing straight at me. I could hear shouts of, 'right on, man' and 'brilliant.' I was in the perfect position as I pulled both steering toggles simultaneously to create the flare and stall the parachute at around 10 feet above the ground. That is the precise point when the wind changed and the wind sock instantly swung in a direction 45 degrees to the left. I could do nothing about it. The stalled parachute flipped on its side and dumped me in, right leg first. I hit the ground and there was an audible crack as my ankle broke. Several jumpers rushed to grab the parachute that was trying to take off again in the wind, to prevent me being dragged along the ground.

'Wow, tough shit man' and 'Holy shit,' rang in my ears, the pain engulfed me and I got to my feet (well foot), supported by Mitch and Roland. My jumping days were over for a while, which was the only upside to this event. I never did get to enjoy this activity.

The only silver lining to this black cloud that unexpectedly terminated my efforts to become a skydiver was the beautiful large breasted, blonde female that was detailed to take me to hospital. En route to that establishment she talked non-stop about my bad luck and similar incidents that she herself had encountered during her five years of jumping out of perfectly serviceable aircrafts. It included a detailed account of the time her boyfriend had a canopy malfunction, which she witnessed from the ground, necessitating the opening of his reserve chute at 400 feet.

'He was just eight seconds under canopy,' she recounted, 'and two seconds away from a deep six. Man, that was hard core to watch,' she sighed as I was wheeled to the x-ray department unsure if she was looking for a reaction or trying to make me realise I was lucky that I was not dead.

The hospital handled the injury in a very routine manner and put my lower right leg into a fibreglass cast. The blonde lady was driving back to the jump site when she noticed me grimacing in pain. The ankle was swelling and, under the cast, it had nowhere to go.

'Do you have any painkillers?' she asked. I told her that they had not given me any and she asked if I wanted one.

'Yes please,' I answered, thinking how well prepared this young lady was – prepared for any eventuality.

'OK,' she said, 'I'll pull over and roll you one.' I was not exactly familiar with these life giving, pain relieving spliffs, but I can report that they do work to some extent. It felt a little better.

Back at the jump site I slumped on to a patch of grass and lay down in the sun to accept the sympathy and well wishes of the crowd. The group was joined by the doctor, also a skydiver, who took out the x-ray pictures and explained, in medical terms, the extent of the damage, the treatment and prognosis, to all those in attendance. It was hot; I was dehydrating and looked over longingly to the vending machine that dispensed ice cold drinks.

The doctor enquired, 'Do you want anything?'

'Coke,' I replied. He personally went off to fetch it and returned five minutes later with a piece of silver foil, which he unwrapped revealing a white powder.

'No,' I protested, 'I need a drink – Coke.' The blonde lady explained that I would be better off with the drug, it would not make the pain go away, exactly, but it would stop me caring about it. I politely declined, honest!

The main problem with this situation was that it meant I could not continue with the training, which was vital. I argued that the right leg was in a fibreglass cast and was probably stronger than the left leg now, so I protested, 'Could I please finish the training?' I had made a reasonable point that was well debated between the doctor and Mitch, but the counter argument was that the leg in the cast was heavier than the other leg. It would hang lower in free fall and may cause spinning that I would be unable to correct. Someone suggested that I have the other leg put in a cast for a couple of days, just to finish the training, but common sense prevailed and Mitch Decoteau signed off my log book with the comment 'a victim of turbulent conditions.' I packed my bags and limped home to the UK.

But the show had to go on and a few days later I was in a one man cloudhopper, leg in a cast, being interviewed by Michael Aspel on his networked TV chat show. We were in the news and on television on a daily basis by this time. News at Ten, the national daily news programme, was covering every aspect of the project. We also appeared on the children's TV programme Blue Peter several times and a variety of other programmes. It was high profile stuff and my two young children, Myles and James, would no longer be seen in my company, regarding it as un-cool for their dad to be so well-known. My youngest son Robert was also making the news as I strapped him to my chest, at the age of six months, and took him for a flight in a cloudhopper with a bottle of gripe water in my hand. He hated it (the cloudhopper not the gripe water).

There had been a long debate on whether we should use a pressurised capsule for the attempt or an open gondola and spacesuits. The main areas of discussion centred on the cost and the inhibited manoeuvrability that the spacesuits would bring to the project. Dexterity is vital when you are trying to save yourself and spacesuits are not great if you have to suddenly leap out of a capsule, pull various levers, pull several switches, including emergency oxygen supplies, pull parachute rip cords – not to mention the necessity to be able to make subtle body and hand movements to control a free fall descent. Spacesuits were also very difficult to obtain and enormously expensive. NASA did fit me with a Dash 7 spacesuit – the same type used for the Apollo missions and I confess that, while they may have been an absolutely critical element of travelling in the Saturn rockets to the moon and orbiting the earth in the vacuum of space, they were not for Operation Sky Quest. With a procurement cost of £150,000 we could not afford them anyway. Per Lindstrand designed the capsule and NASA agreed to run a risk assessment programme. There were several technical areas of which NASA had great experience and this was one of them. A small but critical item that had been developed thanks to space technology was explosive bolts. These needed to be attached to the capsule in order to jettison the huge balloon envelope when we returned to splash down in the ocean. Otherwise, the capsule and its occupants may be dragged along for some time, the capsule filling with sea water and acting like an anchor. Some of NASA's astronauts had lost their lives in this way. Alternatively, if a sea landing was not achieved, the capsule may be dragged bumping along the ground, hitting objects along the way. The NASA explosive bolts were designed with a failure rate of less than 0.1 per cent but again they were very costly. They pointed us to an external manufacturer that only guaranteed a failure rate of one in ten, but at a fraction of the cost.

So a test capsule was built and Per and I attached it to the red Milk's Gotta Lotta Bottle test balloon, with the explosive bolts, donned our pressure suits and parachutes and made several test flights, pressurising and depressurising in flight. These training flights were critical in getting us flight ready and completely familiar with all the on-board systems, check lists and procedures that would have to become second nature to both of us.

The need for planning and procedures, plus a commitment to safety, had to be top priority as any relaxation of those elements could prove catastrophic. A tragic reminder of that was to occur in the following days, when Per telephoned me.

'Have you heard the news?' Per said.

'What news?' I replied.

He told me I should sit down for this and went on to explain that our colleagues, Dick Wirth and Christina Robinson, who worked for him at his balloon manufacturing base in London, had both been burned to death in a horrific balloon accident in Albuquerque, New Mexico. They had died in the worst possible way.

They were invited to jump into a balloon basket by the owner Captain Joe Gonzalez. It was a large Thunder balloon, built at Dick's factory. The balloon was attending the Albuquerque balloon meet, the largest balloon fiesta in the world, with hundreds of aerostats attending. It is an incredible and spectacular event, held annually, with balloonists coming from all over the world to experience a fun-filled week of balloon flying. There was nothing fun-filled about the 1982 balloon meet.

Dick and his seamstress Christina accepted the invitation to fly and climbed into the basket. As the balloon became light and ready for take off, a fuel line ruptured, spewing propane gas into the basket. Joe Gonzalez jumped out immediately and saved himself, the balloon began to rise due to the sudden reduction of weight and sent the balloon into a rapid climb with the remaining passengers, who were quickly engulfed in the inferno. Apparently, Dick jumped out at several hundred feet, preferring to die from the impact of the fall, rather than burning to death. It was a massive blow to ballooning and no one could imagine the emptiness of a balloon field without his infectious enthusiasm and his golden wellington boots that were his trademark. Dick's pals all attended a memorial at St Martins-in-the-Fields church in the heart of London and had a good sing song in his memory. The gold wellington boots were later replicated into an annually awarded trophy which I was honoured to receive for my contribution to ballooning. The old adage, 'plan for an emergency and it will not occur' rang in my ears. The last flight Dick made was unplanned, a spur of the moment event that killed him.

Peter Mason was in my office and declared that he wanted me to take him on a fun flight. No training, nothing formal, just a pleasure flight so he could talk to me about life in general for the book he had been commissioned to write. He had made several flights but said that he really wanted to go above the clouds. It was an ambition of his. I agreed and we scheduled a flight for the following weekend. The weather was forecast to be fine, but with a cloud base at 4,000 feet.

It turned out to be one of the most idyllic and memorable flights I have ever made. We took off from the village of Quatford, close to my home in Bridgnorth. The winds were light and we drifted just north of east towards Ironbridge, over the rolling Shropshire countryside. I explained that I needed to get well into the countryside, away from towns, before we climbed through the cloud. Descending back through clouds can be tricky as you cannot accurately tell how low the cloud will be and how high the ground will be when you break through the cloud base. We drifted over Wenlock Edge where the ground falls away sharply. The wind, flowing over the ridge, creates turbulence which can cause distortion in the envelope, which can slam you into the ground. In early ballooning days, with puny burners and Velcro rips that could open in flight, this was to be avoided at all costs. Nowadays, I explained to Peter, with three burners on board we could handle this 'curl-over' and I purposely set the balloon a few feet above the ridge as the ground dropped steeply. At a distance of about 1,300 feet past the ridge the wind kicked in, the envelope listed over and the fabric caved in, but I was ready for it and quickly refilled the balloon with hot air to fly on. Peter loved it and I put the balloon into a 2,000 feet per minute ascent to climb to the cloud base. We stopped climbing at the cloud base and just hung there with the basket below the cloud and the envelope above us, almost out of sight in the thick vapour. I explained that the cloud was wet, compared to the blue sky below, which is why we had stopped ascending. I would put more heat in to take us aloft. Deep inside the cloud it was silent and our voices took on a muffled tone as we communicated. A minute later we broke through the cloud and into a clear and very bright blue sky, looking over miles of nothing but white cloud tops and without any feeling of movement. Peter was mesmerised as we danced around the sky. Dipping the balloon in and out of the cloud valleys and climbing the cloud mountains, pushing through the trails of vapour that seemed to reach out to the envelope in an effort to embrace us as we flew on. We stayed 'on top' for twenty minutes before I re-entered the clouds to make a descent.

I demonstrated to Peter how we used to gauge the rise and fall of the balloon before the advent of instruments that gave us that information. Once deep in the cloud, in the early days of ballooning, it was difficult to estimate the descent speed and we needed to keep it slow so we could use the burners to stop quickly when we came back through, in case the ground, or any tall obstacle, was immediately below us. We would tear up small pieces of paper and throw them out of the basket to watch them rise in order to estimate the rate of descent until the ground became visible again.

We broke through the cloud base revealing below us the glorious Severn Valley, with the river running east towards the historic Iron Bridge, lying in the centre of the town named after it. We were now heading west but I knew that if I got into the valley, near to the surface, the wind would change direction and would be flowing down the valley. I made the descent and went right down to the surface of the river, placing the basket on the water, the current taking the balloon, Peter and I towards the historic town of Ironbridge. We chatted to anglers on each side of the river bank as we slowly floated past. They did not mention, or seem to mind, that we may be disturbing the fish or interrupting their afternoon. It was strangely ridiculous but stunning and uncompromisingly simple and I switched the burner on to leave the river and climb gently over the famous bridge.

The town of Ironbridge is rather beautiful from any perspective, but particularly so from a bird's eye view at 1,000 feet above it. We both spoke to the many tourists that were visiting the town as we flew by and rose to 1,500 feet to catch the easterly wind again.

I looked towards the horizon and saw a crop circle about a mile away. We were both excited but the current direction would take us away from it. I immediately took the balloon back up to the cloud base which turned the balloon direction to the right of the crop circle. Knowing the direction of the wind on the surface I waited until we were in the right position and descended very quickly to catch the surface wind that would take us in the right direction. That manoeuvre is not always achievable but, that day, it was. Perfect.

We drifted right over the crop circle at 10 feet above the ground and talked to the people who were standing in the middle of it.

'When did this appear?' I asked as we floated past.

'This morning,' came the reply, adding, 'did you do it? Where have you come from?' Some things never change.

I climbed again to decide where to land and Peter looked out of the basket commenting, 'This has been absolutely magical. One of the most fabulous things I have ever done, beautiful English countryside and wonderful company.'

I told him it may get better yet and quoted my favourite poem . . .
'Oh to be on England,
Now that April's there,
For whoever lives in England,
See the summer, unaware,
That the tiny bud, around the Elm tree bowl is in tiny leaf,
And the Chaffinch sings on the orchard bough,
In England, now.'

A bastardisation of the classic Robert Browning poem but it is how I recalled it.

I briefed him that I was planning to land in ten minutes, having spotted the most perfect of landing spots.

'Do you need to tell the crew?' asked Peter (we now had air to ground radios).

'It's not necessary, they'll know where I'm landing,' I replied.

'How?' said Peter but I did not answer. I had spotted the retrieve crew on a main road just behind me and they knew the area and knew me well enough to anticipate where I was about to land. I let the balloon descend and flew low over a wheat field, brushing the ears of the crop as we floated towards a group of buildings. It was the Acton Arms pub, which I knew well, and I clipped the hedge and landed softly in the car park and into the hands of the crew. We stood there for a few minutes while the crew brought out two pints of cool, real ale. A perfect end to a perfect flight.

Peter Mason became a great friend and left journalism to learn to skydive and open up his own ballooning company, but his roots were in writing and storytelling. He told me a story which I will always remember; one of the funniest things I have ever heard. It relates to a fellow journalist who, whilst attending a very highbrow party, became hopelessly drunk. As he got up from a sofa he knocked over a priceless Ming vase and smashed it. The following day he could not remember anything and was called in by his editor. When the situation was explained by the editor the man was beside himself with anger at his stupidity and embarrassment. He decided to go to the house to make his apologies and try to compensate the owner.

He was met at the door by the lady of the house who was unsurprisingly upset and very curt. He made an abject apology, explaining he was deeply ashamed of his behaviour. He even offered to pay for the damage. The lady explained, quietly but sternly, that this vase was one of a pair and was priceless and compensation was not an option. He was eventually asked in and given a cup of tea, but the atmosphere was very cold indeed. He sat on a sofa, well adorned with numerous cushions, contrite and deeply ashamed, constantly glancing to the left of him at the empty stand, now devoid of its rare and priceless vase. On his right hand side, with worrying isolation, stood the remaining (and arguably even rarer) vase sitting on top of its stand. He was so nervous he could not drink his tea as his hands were shaking so much and he felt terrifyingly close to the one remaining vase.

Thinking it was the right time to leave he nervously rose to his feet. As he stood up he turned slightly to navigate away from the remaining vase and noticed something on the sofa. He had sat on the lady's Pekinese dog and suffocated it. It was quite dead. Apparently, he shouted, 'Oh shit!' and ran out of the house wailing.

So Peter left this life behind him and joined us as our official biographer for the Operation Sky Quest project that offered the opportunity to enjoy many more tales of adventure.

Chapter Fourteen

Dreams to Nightmares at the Edge of Space

The capsule training and systems analysis were progressing well. We had to train to be able to operate the capsule systems blindfold, and did so. There were many sessions with Per and I sitting in the pressurised capsule with visors down and all visibility blacked out. There was always a real possibility that the interior of the capsule would become fogged out and we had to learn the precise location of every switch, instrument and handle in case we found ourselves flying blind.

The whole basis of this attempt was to be able to build a balloon that could climb very quickly, ascending at a rate close to 4,000 feet per minute. The shape of a conventional balloon (inverted tear drop) is not really built to climb or descend rapidly and the altitude balloon would need a more aerodynamic shape to be able to achieve this. We built a small replica balloon for test purposes so the final shape of the attempt balloon could be refined and determined. The test balloon could only carry a single pilot and was built with ultra light materials. The basket was constructed in carbon fibre with very fine wires connecting to the burner frame which, itself was constructed with lightweight alloys containing a single burner.

Flying this replica was rather daunting since it lacked any of the psychological security of the more robustly built hot air balloons and I found it an unpleasant task. I did not like flying solo at the best of times but these test flights had to be done. I donned a helmet, together with a parachute, and took the balloon for is first test flight.

Once at 1,000 feet (enough height to parachute from) I applied more heat from the burner and initiated a climb rate of 2,500 feet per minute. The balloon behaved correctly and climbed in a stable manner. I then opened the burners for a 30 second burn and waited. The balloon began to climb very rapidly, accelerating, twisting and eventually going across the sky at a very odd angle. I could do nothing to stop this at all and I confess I elected to sit on the basket floor, holding onto the rim until the balloon stabilized. It eventually stopped zipping around at odd angles and I let it fall slowly and safely, applying measured burns to control the descent. It was a horrible thing to fly and I delegated further flights to the stand in pilot, Tom Donnelly. He experienced similar situations in the replica balloon and revealed that he too, at times, cowered in the bottom of the basket, scared out of his wits. However, it was an important element of the test programme and eventually determined the final shape of the attempt balloon.

The water ditching was also a vital part of the flight plan. When the capsule landed in the sea, a carefully planned rescue would swing into place. A diving team had been training, led by my close friend, and experienced diver, David Omerod. They knew the plan well and had committed themselves to the project and now needed to practice this vital part of the programme, in real time. The capsule was designed to float and the plan was that Per and I would land with the capsule already depressurised and the door open. If it went according to plan we would wait on the water until they came to get us. The divers would be following the last few miles of the flight in a search and rescue helicopter. The dive team had to assume the worst case scenario, namely Per and I being unconscious with the capsule still pressurised. In that case they would need to pull a lever on the outside of the capsule to depressurise the pod in order to get the door open and pull us out. Alternatively, the door may be open and we may be in imminent danger of sinking. The critical factor was that the divers should be right with us at the moment of impact with the water. They would jump into the sea from the helicopter and get us out. It needed practice and we all assembled at a reservoir called Stoney Cove in Leicestershire for a test run. The news cameras were there, of course, as well as the project television documentary film crew. The plan was for me to take my seat in the capsule, which would be pressurised, and a helicopter would carry me to the middle of the lake and drop me into the water. The height of the drop was measured to simulate the maximum speed of the anticipated landing, and calculations suggested it would only need a height of 15 feet to achieve this. Even at that height the impact from a dead drop would be hard. The test had to be precise and finely timed. Dropping me from any height above 20 feet could prove nasty and cause injury. The consequences of a drop from 30 feet or above were well understood. It could kill me.

Per was to be in control of the drop, standing on the lake shore and being in communication with the helicopter pilot who would only release the payload on his instruction.

Before the lift the capsule was floated on the water and the divers familiarised themselves with it and practiced decompressing the capsule and dragging me out to a dinghy. Once they were satisfied David Omerod gave the clearance for the lift. But not before publicity pictures were taken as required by the sponsor, the Milk Marketing Board. This entailed me donning a diving suit and being taken to the bottom of the lake, where an aircraft wreck was lying. We were asked to sit in the cockpit and simulate the drinking of a pint of milk for which a glass, painted to look as though it contained milk, had been provided. A diver/cameraman took the photograph to provide the sponsors with a picture they could use with a press release. It had to be done, the sponsors were spending a lot of money on this project.

We were finally ready and I climbed on board, performed all of the capsule checks and gave the signal to lift-off. I was completely in the hands of the helicopter pilot and Per. I confess to being slightly nervous. This needed to be precise.

As predicted, I could hear the radio chat, through my headphones but was unable to communicate back to either the ground or the helicopter as my transmissions could not break through the noise of the static and helicopter engines. The pilot flew to the centre of the lake and I heard the confirmation that the divers were in place and ready. I could see that the helicopter was hovering above the calculated height and I heard the pilot ask for instructions and the order to release. It transpired that the film crew heard this request and issued a radio message that they were ready for the release.

I heard, 'Release now,' and I knew we were far too high.

I frantically pushed the transmit button and shouted, 'Too high! Too high!' but they could not hear me. I felt the pilot adjust the height a little, thank God, and then the inevitable shudder as the release mechanism was activated.

'Relax, relax,' went through my mind as I went in a dead drop on to the surface of the water. This practice session now became a real situation. The bottom of the capsule was convex in shape and it hit the surface like hitting concrete, staving in the bottom of the capsule and ripping the instrument panel off the fixings, depositing it on to my lap. I was in a sitting position for the impact and I blacked out for a few seconds, regaining consciousness with an acute pain in my back and a very fuzzy feeling in my head. I could do nothing but wait to be pulled out. I saw the divers peering in at the window as they were depressurising the capsule. They gave me an, 'are you OK?' sign by forming a circle with their thumb and forefinger and saw me respond with the same signal. They managed to open the door and drag me out of the capsule and into the dinghy. My legs would not work properly and my ears were ringing, but I thought I was OK and the medics checked me out on the shore.

The capsule was a write-off but it wasn't a major problem as Per had built it as a test platform and its loss would not slow the project down. I was incredibly grateful to the helicopter pilot. His instinct had told him that we were too high and his last second adjustment had probably saved my life. Per calculated that I had gone through a 15-17 G force. Any more than that could have been catastrophic. It seems that the impact had compressed my spine and bruised the kidneys while my brain had bounced around in the cranial cavity. It was not pleasant.

Some weeks later, still working through the effects of the incident, I saw the NASA flight surgeon at the Johnson Space Centre in Houston, Texas, who wanted to review my condition. He told me I was going to feel those effects for 12 months. He was right.

On the project schedule was the need for us to undertake some high altitude flights in an open basket and fully kitted out in the flight pressure suits, oxygen masks and parachutes. This would mean that Per and I, while standing next to each other during the flight, would only be able to communicate via the on-board radio. We took off from Oswestry, steadily climbing at 1,000 feet per minute. Part of this trial flight was to determine the level at which the burners would stop functioning due to the lack of oxygen at high altitudes. The burners would have to be relit and various items were carried to make sure this was achievable. This included a spark gun – a conventional gas lighter – and a specific type of match with a very long fuse that, once struck, would burn through for several seconds. They were big matches, housed in a large box, which could be accessed even with my gloved hands. They were placed strategically in the basket and it would be a simple matter to extract them from the holder, strike and attempt to relight the burners. The film crew were recording and tracking this flight from the ground using a camera with a very long telescopic lens.

We climbed slowly up to 40,000 feet, where the temperature was down to minus 40 degrees in the clear blue sky, when we both had a little panic. I observed large clear flakes falling from the envelope. Per had spotted them as well and we both looked around the balloon for some explanation. My immediate concern was that the coating of the fabric of the balloon envelope was separating and the consequences of that were not attractive. It was then I realised that Per, in moments of stress, thought and spoke in his native Swedish language.

I pressed my radio button and, as calmly as possible, said, 'Per, any idea what this stuff is?'

He pressed his radio button, looking straight at me, and said something like 'oobi doobie doo, hurdie gurdie wurdie…'

I pressed the radio button again and said, 'Per, you're speaking Swedish,' adding with a little more urgency, 'speak English!'

At that moment a large flake landed on my glove and as I rubbed it to inspect it properly I realised that it was ice, there were tons of it cascading around the basket. Per was observing this and spoke to me again, this time in a nervous mixture of Swedish and English.

His voice came over the radio and into my earphones, 'Oobi doobie – vapour trail.'

We were indeed climbing quite quickly and were producing a trail of vapour, similar to the white lines in the sky produced by the large airliners. I don't think this phenomenon had ever been experienced before by a hot air balloon. We contacted the ground crew who confirmed that this was indeed happening and visible, quite clearly, from the ground.

To his embarrassment, I often told this story of Per's communications in Swedish and we joked about it a lot. He would always finish the tale by adding that a few minutes later the burners did expire and I used one of the special matches to reignite them. The match was still burning after the burners were functioning again and Per recalls that I put it to my mouth to blow it out. Of course, I was in a pressure suit with oxygen mask and my visor fogged up immediately. When the mist cleared I could see that Per was standing in the corner of the basket shaking with laughter. Touché.

So we were now as near to flight ready as we could be and a date for the operation was scheduled. We were to take off from RAF Watton in Norfolk and the RAF was supporting the flight with helicopters for the anticipated sea landing. There was a massive amount of press on site. It seemed that everything we did was in full view of the media – warts and all. A media centre was installed and hundreds of journalists were in attendance to see the launch. It was going out live on national television.

I walked through the media centre, late one evening before we were scheduled to lift-off, and was disconcerted to see one of the journalists writing my obituary – just in case. It was a sobering thought but I was aware of the dangers. I printed off a copy and still have it to this day. Even my wife, with baby Robert in her arms, was interviewed by the national news – to her abject horror – and asked if she thought we would make it without killing ourselves. She calmly informed them that we had completed all of the training and thought that we would be fine.

We were worried about the weather. The cloud base had got very low and the surface wind was picking up. We needed calm conditions to inflate this 264 feet tall monster balloon and stable weather on the ground to complete all of the checks before lift-off. The weather deteriorated by the minute. The surface wind across the airfield was at the maximum allowed for take off and the winds aloft were getting stronger. Importantly, the sea conditions were forecast to get rough, making a safe sea landing difficult. There was no doubt that the flight had to be postponed. The world was watching and we made a decision to call off the flight but still inflate the balloon so that the press would, at least, have some pictures to file with the story of the postponement. The sponsors were anxious to get some good exposure and it would be good practice for the inflation crew. So the inflation went ahead. It was a dreadful mistake. The press would get their story but it was not the one we wanted them to publish.

The balloon was rolled out and the inflation fans switched on to begin filling the envelope with cold air. The capsule was moved into position. I was being interviewed by a television crew when the ambulance raced past me, across the field, blue lights flashing and sirens screaming. Richard Down, the project co-ordinator, pulled me away from the TV crew and told me there had been an accident. Per had been at the crown of the balloon when the wind on the surface had veered suddenly and he had been taken off his feet, falling on his back from a height of 20 feet. I was staggered that Per had broken the first rule of ballooning, 'Don't let your feet get off the ground' (unless you are in the gondola).

I went to see him, before the medic tried to move him, and saw that the balloon envelope was under great strain from the wind shear. As I stooped down to speak to Per there was a loud ripping noise as the balloon envelope split. Per was in pain but philosophical and smiling with the irony of it all. He had held onto the crown rope, the wind shear had kicked in and he was launched into the air without time to react.

Unfortunately the whole event was filmed and aired on the national news that evening. The sponsors were sympathetic but not amused.

The only funny side to this story was an argument that took place between the two ambulance crews that had attended the incident. The St John paramedic and the NHS ambulance crew were arguing about whose patient Per was, the St John crew claiming that they were first on the scene and that the NHS were trying to steal their patient. Richard Down pointed out that he did not care whose patient it was, the important thing was to get Per to hospital quickly. Although in great discomfort Per's eyes were gleaming with the amusement at it all, as he was loaded into one of the ambulances and transported to hospital. It transpired that he had damaged his back and arm and it would be some weeks before he was fit to fly again.

The delay would have serious consequences for the project. We had lost the weather slot for the next few weeks and with the oncoming of autumn, then winter, it would mean that the project would have to be postponed until the following season. This would be a bad blow, we did not have the budget for this delay and would need to raise more money. It was always going to be difficult to fly this project from the UK and the weather research indicated that only four or five slots per year were going to be available in prevailing conditions to inflate and fly the mission. A delay in the project was inevitable, but at least it would provide time for Per to recover. There was little point in asking the third pilot to stand in for Per. He was strong and would be fit and fully recovered by the time we were ready for the next attempt. After much deliberation we decided that, reluctantly, we would have to look for climates with predicable and forecastable weather conditions and abandon our attempts to fly this all-British project from the UK.

Operation Sky Quest was a high profile mission and Richard Down secured additional sponsorship from the breakfast cereal manufacture and food giant Kellogg's. The Milk Marketing Board retained the signage on the balloon but Kellogg's was a good sub-sponsor. Milk and breakfast cereal went well together! The balloon was repaired at Per's Oswestry factory and the Kellogg's logo was stitched onto the balloon. We were off to Arizona where winds were light and conditions aloft were often stable. It seemed the perfect launch area and we moved the entire team and all of the equipment to a small town called Page on the Utah/Arizona border. We hired a light aircraft and Per and I flew on the projected downwind flight path to survey the landing area. There were large lakes in the immediate vicinity so the diving crew was still needed. Again, in the event of landing in the water we would need them to get us out quickly. The rest of the downwind terrain was mostly desert, not as soft as the water but acceptable. We retired to our hotel accommodation on the edge of Lake Powell and waited for a good weather slot.

The day for take off had finally arrived and we announced that the project status had moved from red to amber. We went to green late in the evening after confirming that the weather forecast was suitable and moved the inflation crews, diving team, medics, emergency teams and helicopter retrieve crew into place. A small tethered blimp was deployed with nylon streamers placed every 30 feet, as wind indicators, and the inflation got underway. Per and I were moved to a temporary building, installed for this project, next to the launch area to begin pre-breathing of oxygen. We had to saturate our lungs with oxygen for an hour before the flight. We sat there watching the process. It was acceptable to be nervous, that kept you alert, but I was suddenly overcome with a feeling of great foreboding. I knew that in a matter of minutes I would be entering the capsule and I had a premonition that if I did that I would die in the process of making this record attempt. I wanted to stop the process right now. I considered backing out at this late stage but came to the conclusion that I would prefer to accept the risk of getting killed, rather than calling it off. It was a conscious decision and I was resigned to whatever fate had in store.

We waited to be called to the capsule as I watched one of my pilots, Peter Tilney, take a cloudhopper to the top of the now fully inflated balloon to inspect the explosive panel at the top. The panel was a two metre diameter piece of fabric that we would blow out at the top of the climb. It would leave a hole in the balloon which would let out the hot air and bring us back to earth. The hole was essential to the descent. Apart from the burners, the air inside the envelope would heat up from the solar energy produced by the sun. We did not know if the natural cooling of the balloon would be sufficient to bring the balloon down quickly enough and we had a limited eight hour supply of oxygen.

Peter Tilney inspected the explosive panel and began his descent back to the surface. As he touched down - all was correct. The inflation crew for the huge balloon were making final checks and attaching the flying wire to the capsule when one of the wires caught on a fuel line. It ruptured immediately and the crew went into a well-practiced emergency procedure, evacuating the site. Per and I were on our feet walking to the capsule when the propane gas fuel tanks blew clouds of propane out over the launch area. In a procedure rehearsed many times, we were grabbed and thrown into a vehicle, on standby for that eventuality, which drove us, lying prone, to a safe position. We watched aghast as the balloon ripped from its moorings and took off without us. It was a devastating moment. The culmination of two years of work had gone in seconds, along with our aspirations, ambitions, hopes and prayers. I climbed out of the vehicle and watched the envelope rising above the Arizona desert, flying to an unknown destination, without us. I stood there and, I confess, I cried. I don't know whether it was from disappointment, relief or anger. Perhaps a little of each.

The NASA personnel were philosophical about it, 'Look,' they said, 'you did everything right and nobody's dead.' It was of little consolation. NASA had experienced failures and several deaths during its long and illustrious history and was used to dealing with the odd failure amongst its many successes. We all knew the risks. 'Just pick yourself up and start again, you're doing great work,' they commented, but I knew it was over, at least for the time being. We were out of money and the sponsors were unwilling to supply more cash. The town of Page rallied around us and even made attempts to raise the cash we needed for another attempt at the record. In the end we had no alternative but to pack our bags and go back to the UK feeling deflated – much like our balloon.

We later learned that my premonition of impending doom had some merit. Per asked a group of Swedish air force scientists to do some calculations and they determined that the explosive panel at the top would have made little difference. The solar heating would have kept us at altitude for many hours, until the sun went down. We would have been out of oxygen and would have needed to jump out of the capsule. We all knew the probable consequences of that.

It was a failure but, in some ways, a glorious failure. When you embark on this type of ambitious project you not only have to accept the personal risks to your health and welfare, but also the risk of public failure. You place your head above the parapet and understand that you may well get shot at. Most of the press were sympathetic and supportive but some did criticise the efforts that we had made. We understood and accepted both points of view.

It was time to go back to work. We had to pitch for a major new client, Virgin. This was a big piece of new business and I wanted the contract, very badly. I was, however, going to be up against stiff and professional competition in the form of Colin Prescott of the Hot Air Balloon Company, known as HabCo. I had had my fill with failing and would throw everything into this presentation. Failure was not an option. I was determined to win.

I was to face yet another, even greater, disappointment.

Chapter Fifteen

Like a Virgin

The Virgin business was important to me. I knew of Richard Branson and his success in Virgin Records and that he had recently started an airline called Virgin Atlantic, with daily flights to New York from Gatwick. His management team had contacted us and wanted ideas on how to promote the brand new airline. Hugh Band, Virgin Atlantics' marketing director, was an innovator in the airline business, probably because he had absolutely no experience of the airline industry, and was brought in by Richard to think outside of the box.

Hugh had insisted on the Virgin aircraft livery being different to other airlines and that the aircraft were to be painted white, including the belly of the Boeing 747. This added weight to the planes and was resisted by the engineering teams, but he got his way. He also introduced live entertainment acts on board, which also meant less room for fare paying passengers. However, it provided for a different and exciting product that stood out from the crowd. The airline was launched in a blaze of publicity and was immediately supported by the air travelling public. Hugh, led by Richard, took controversial decisions that were unpopular with some of the traditional airline operatives. These ideas included the on-board screening of air disaster type films that some of the management team thought inappropriate, but Richard's instinct told him the market wanted a fresh and different flight experience. Most of Hugh's ideas were implemented, in spite of opposition from his contemporaries, and Virgin Atlantic provided a new, friendly product which delivered an on-board service that was different and, most importantly, created an atmosphere of excitement and fun which appealed greatly to the passengers and gave it a marketing edge. Virgin Atlantic did not have a 'first class' service. It offered an 'upper class' ticket which was similar to other airlines' business class and an economy ticket that Richard wanted to call 'riff raff' but was advised against it.

My company, Lighter Than Air Ltd, worked hard to get this business. I thought it had the potential to develop into a major account. It had our name written all over it – or so I thought. Hugh Band was very up front with me and informed us that we were in competition with two other concerns, one of which was my old adversary, Colin Prescott and the Hot Air Balloon Company.

We came up with various innovative ideas and I was a nervous wreck waiting while Hugh deliberated on who should be awarded the contract. I was devastated when Hugh informed me that we had not got the business. It had gone to my arch rival, lock, stock and basket. I watched with anger and disappointment as the contract was announced with details of the balloons Virgin had commissioned. One of the balloons was a great piece of design, a regular balloon shape, art worked in a cloud and sky design, with a Boeing 747 flying through it. The wings, cockpit and tail of the aircraft were built on to the envelope in a stunning piece of balloon construction design. It reflected the airline philosophy of unique innovation and I seethed at the huge lost opportunity – but not for long.

It also became apparent that Richard was captivated by the whole ballooning experience and was going to learn to fly. To make matters worse, Richard had announced that he was going to attempt to fly the Atlantic with Per Lindstrand. Much of the experience and technology obtained in the Operation Sky Quest project would be put to good use. It would involve building a pressurised capsule attached to a massive hot air balloon, capable of flying in the jet stream at great speed. In attempting to fly the Atlantic there were two options. The first was to fly at comparatively low altitudes, like previous attempts, which meant a slow passage subject to normal weather conditions. The alternative was to fly above the weather, at 30,000 feet, entering the jet stream. The jet stream is a very fast band of wind, moving at speeds of over 200 miles per hour.

The advantage of a low level flight was that it was relatively inexpensive and low tech undertaking and could be achieved in an open basket or gondola. The much respected pioneer of modern hot air balloon flight, Don Cameron of Bristol based Cameron Balloons, had already attempted such a flight and had almost succeeded. The alternative transatlantic balloon flight was an expensive, high tech approach, with a pressurised capsule and flying in the jet stream at speeds far in excess of anything ever tried before. Typically, Richard decided to go for the jet stream approach. High cost, high tech and high risk. It was a bold and ambitious plan.

The flight involved almost everything I had previously trained for and I watched with envy as Richard began accelerated free fall parachute training. However, he was not very good at it. On two occasions he pulled the wrong rip cord – opening the reserve parachute – jettisoning the main chute. He was philosophical and casual about this while terrifying his Royal Marine instructors who feared losing an important, high profile business celebrity.

I was determined to get another shot at winning this business. While my envious eyes watched the Virgin balloon programme gather momentum, Hugh Band left the company to join one of their competitors, Continental Airlines, as marketing director. Continental Airlines was a big carrier, based out of Texas, and had a chequered financial history. It was re-launching with a new brand and the company was keen to protect its highly valued London to New York route. Continental believed that Virgin was a threat to that business sector and desperately wanted to protect it. Hugh wanted to promote the company brand, create loyalty with the frequent flyer base and stimulate interest in the airline. He called me.

A major promotional tour was being scheduled, starting with a road show around Scotland. It was an exciting programme that took in all of the major towns and cities and presented the airline as a dynamic force in the business and holiday travel sectors of the market.

The travelling road show, complete with a dance troupe, a festival of music and entertainment would, the company hoped, present the airline with a new, up to date, dynamic image that would appeal to seasoned travellers.

As I anticipated, Hugh wanted to make a statement for Continental Airlines and commissioned a large gold balloon with the Continental logo emblazoned across both sides. The balloon was stunning, built in a shiny gold fabric that would be a high impact promotional tool to supplement the Scottish tour and provide great press and TV opportunities for the balloons.

I would accompany the tour to co-ordinate the press and TV activity, offering flights to selected journalists. I appointed Peter Tilney to pilot the balloon and recruited a local lad, Colin Thomas, to act as ground crew.

I liked Colin from the moment I met him. He was young, strong and not averse to hard work. He had been a handful in his teens, gotten himself into a lot of trouble and had recently come out of Shrewsbury prison, after being arrested and convicted of grievous bodily harm. His fighting prowess was legendary around Bridgnorth, where he was referred to as 'The Bulldog'. He was frequently arrested for some affray and spent a lot of weekends in the police cells. The local bobby told me it used to take six coppers to arrest Colin after a night on the beer but, amazingly, they all seemed to like him. They told me he needed a chance to prove himself.

After 13 convictions, fines, probation and a spell in jail, Colin became one of my crew. Despite his history, or maybe because of it, Colin and I became friends and that has endured to this day. He is entirely trustworthy, reliable and loyal.

I later taught him to fly. He had never passed an exam in his life, but became a very good pilot indeed. This young man moved from being a bit of a yob to becoming a useful and valued member of society who travelled the world both working hard and enjoying himself.

My role in the Continental promotional tour was purely administrative as I was carrying an injury from an accident suffered a few weeks prior. Fresh from the Alpine Challenge tour in St Moritz, where I had learned to ski, I was taking my three-year-old son Robert down a dry ski slope in Telford. We collapsed in a heap at the bottom of the slope but the little finger on my left hand got trapped under the dry slope and as we gambolled over it snapped off. I stood up to examine the damage and looked at the remaining stump with the grey bone poking out. I turned over my hand to find my finger lying on the back of it near my watch. Instinctively I picked it up and placed it on the stump as Robert, looking up at me, started to cry. Being a responsible parent, I looked down at him, holding my bloody hand in the air and reassured him, 'Don't cry Rob, daddy will be fine, but I have to go to the hospital straight away.'

Rob looked up at me, examined the stump, started to cry again and said, 'No! I wanted another go on the ski slope!'

So with my left hand out of action I was unable to participate in the actual flying of the balloon. It was a great tour though and Hugh and I started to hatch out a cunning plan.

We both understood the branding power of hot air balloons. While a message on a balloon could not be considered as persuasive – there was no call to action which would convince the consumer to try a new product – there was no doubt that balloons had a very high recall factor. The public recalled, or remembered, seeing a hot air balloon. Perhaps this was because it was high on the… 'I want to do list,' making it aspirational. Perhaps it was simply the boldness of the statement, seeing a name on this unusual vehicle, drifting by. The inescapable fact was that, above all other point of sale and product promotional material, hot air balloons made an impact and that impact remained in the minds of the people that saw it.

Hugh and I also believed that this form of promotion could also become persuasive if it was linked to a marketing drive that offered the public an opportunity to fly in a balloon and to win competitions that offered prizes – like a ticket to New York! From a cost point of view a balloon promotion needed to offer clients value for money. A client could choose to run advertising campaigns in the press or on TV at a known cost. We decided that the market needed a planned schedule that would support a balloon tour, offering the client both press and TV exposure that could be quantified in terms of results achieved. Balloons were press magnets and column inches obtained would need to be valued in terms of audience impacts per thousand. I felt that all hot air balloon campaigns needed a professional public relations effort behind them to maximise publicity and justify the spend, statistically, against traditional forms of sales promotion and advertising

We would offer a complete package and measure the publicity effects of a promotional tour. Not only estimating the value of the balloon being seen live by the public, but by estimating the value of all of the press and TV coverage. We knew that there were known costs of press advertising and, in general, the value of press articles were considered two or three times the value of paid for advertising. The classic phrase described an advertisement with the client saying good things about the product it owned, while an editorial comment was a third party (the journalist) saying good things about the product. It was simple maths. Measure the column inches the balloons attract, estimate what it would cost if the client bought the same amount in advertising space and use a multiple to reach a value received. We conceived a term CPTAIR (The Cost Per Thousand Audience Impact Ratio). The cost of audience impact per thousand in traditional media advertising could vary from as high as £30 per thousand in Sunday glossy magazines, to below £3 on a large television campaign. We reasoned that we could get the CPTAIR down to a few pence with a well planned hot air balloon promotional tour, backed by a PR campaign, it would be an offering that media buyers would be forced to evaluate.

It was to be a new 'total service' company that would legitimise hot air balloon promotions and offer clients a new and exciting medium that would be colourful, memorable and, above all, great fun. Hugh also shared my vision that airships were an important aspect in the future of our company. Although there were only a handful of airships around the world, I knew and believed in the potential of these dirigibles. They were logistical nightmares and hugely expensive to operate with many 'barriers to entry,' as the professional investors would refer to it, but our enthusiasm would find a way of dealing with that.

The name of the new business was going to be important and we felt that it should be simple and clearly state the activities of the company. In other words, do what it says on the tin. The Airship and Balloon Company Ltd was formed. It was going to take some money to set up the new company and it would need an investor with vision, a risk-taking entrepreneur that saw solutions rather than problems. Hugh said, 'I'll give Richard a call.'

Hugh thought that my company, Lighter Than Air Ltd, could be expanded and wanted to approach Richard Branson to invest in the project, using the Virgin brand.

He arranged the meeting with Richard at his Holland Park house and, slightly apprehensive and a little nervous, I boarded a train at Wolverhampton station bound for London Euston. It was a time when the Irish troubles were in full swing and the IRA had taken the fight to London with almost daily parcel bomb alerts.

Hugh and I had prepared our business plan for Richard and I went through this on the train, for the umpteenth time, trying to anticipate deep, penetrating and analytical questions from this famously successful entrepreneur, businessman and visionary. And I must be ready with the answers, without hesitation and with the complete authority and confidence that he would expect. That was utter bollocks – as I was soon to find out.

Richard greeted us warmly. He obviously liked Hugh whom, I later learned, he credited as playing a pivotal part of the definition of the Virgin Atlantic product. I remember looking at this man with rather long hair, wide grin and mandatory sloppy, out of fashion sweater; that looked like it had been knitted by his granny. He shook Hugh's hand warmly and said, 'I wondered how long it would take you to come back to us, you bastard.'

There was no deep or analytical questioning. Richard stretched himself out on a couch and thumbed through the business plan for a few minutes, threw it on an adjoining coffee table and said, 'Ok, let's do it!' He arose from the couch and with an even wider grin shook my hand as the door bell rang followed by a very loud and urgent knocking.

We all moved very quickly to the entrance hall, Hugh and I following Richard to see what on earth the racket was about. Richard stopped suddenly, 'Christ,' he said, staring at a parcel that had been placed in the doorway. It was wrapped in brown paper and about 12 inches wide and eight inches deep. It had a sticker on it with skull and crossbones, oddly printed in green ink. 'Christ,' he repeated.

'Don't touch it,' Hugh said, as Richard moved tentatively towards the package.

'Bloody hell!' I said.

'Fuck,' said Richard, adding, 'what is it?' Richard was furtively edging closer to the package until he was hovering above it. Hugh had gone very quiet and was looking pale. I was remonstrating with myself for getting involved with such a maniac – the thought of launching an international balloon company having retreated to the rearmost recesses of my mind. Richard was now stooping over the package, trying to read the label.

'What's to read?' I thought – it's an effing skull and crossbones!!! I tried to say in the authoritative and clear manner of a natural leader, 'Don't get any closer. It might be a bomb.' However, all that came out was an inaudible squeaky stifled gasp. I tried again, 'Don't touch it!' as Richards's hands moved inextricably towards the package and lifted it off the floor.

Paralysed with fear, Hugh and I watched as the inevitable would surely happen. Richard lifted the parcel delicately and suddenly spun round and shouted, 'BANG!' while kicking the door and throwing the parcel in our direction.

Hugh flattened himself against the wall emitting a strangled cry and went very red. Then he tuned white.

I shit my pants.

Richard was hysterical in laughter, and looking at the state Hugh and I were in became convulsed to a point where he was sobbing and unable to breathe properly.

Hugh was now a better colour – if green is a better colour. He was still pinned against the wall muttering, over and over, 'fucking hell, fucking hell, fucking hell.' Richard slapped him on the shoulder and produced a box of tissues to wipe his tears away. He handed me one and I waddled off to the toilet, like a duck.

The suspect package turned out to be a mail shot to the rich and famous on behalf of a new night club that was opening in the area.

This tendency of Richard's to play practical jokes on people was to become an integral part of our relationship over the next twenty years. Although he did not get it all his own way.

We were to form a relationship that built the largest aerial advertising company on the planet. It involved world record attempts in balloons and airships that would take us to all the corners of the earth. From Japan to the wilderness of northern Canada in game changing hot air balloon flights, to hot air balloon flights in the Valley of the Kings in Egypt and the first paid passenger rides for decades in airship flights over the Las Vegas Stip. We carried out pioneering record flights over Morocco and China and the war-torn Middle East, negotiating safe passages with Colonel Gaddafi, previous and current British Prime Ministers and China's national leaders. It would include playing great pranks on the British press and public, my crossing of Australia in a hot air balloon and operating the largest fleet of airships in the world. There were some great success stories with unbelievable attainments. It was not without its share of failures either in both business and personal terms.

I was to become the Flight Director of the Trans-Pacific attempt, the full facts of which have never been disclosed. I performed the same function for Richards's attempts to be the first to fly a balloon around the world. These two projects were not only very high profile, but very high pressure as I had to make decisions that would either keep the crew safe or result in a loss of their lives.

During such a relationship one can get very close to people, as I did with Richard. I was responsible for his life and during those times I saw the real man. We spent a great deal of time together during the planning of those great projects and I saw how he made life changing decisions affecting the flights and the Virgin businesses, some of which I was intimately involved with – although not all of which I agreed with.

I saw Richard at his best and at his worst. We went on to laugh together in the sheer enjoyment of the tasks we were pursuing in business, record breaking flights and our personal affairs. We also wept together at the tragedies we encountered along the way. It was a mind boggling journey with its fair share of successes, huge risks and a healthy degree of good old fashioned 'cock ups'.

If you enjoyed *Thursday's Child* please look out for the explosive follow-up non-fictional novel – *The Branson Years*.

The Branson Years
[short extract]

Written by Mike Kendrick & Simon W. Golding

One of the first projects for the Airship and Balloon Company was a commitment to share the lighter than air experience with everyone who had a desire to fly in a balloon. As soon as Richard had completed the crossing of the Atlantic and established a host of new world records he was as committed as I was to make the experience available to everyone. You could be forgiven for thinking that he may have been put off balloons for life, having narrowly missed killing himself. I talked to him a lot about this and his innermost thoughts as he was contemplating almost certain death. I read the hastily scribbled notes he had written to his wife Joan and children, Holly and Sam, before he had unexpectedly found himself alone in the balloon at 10,000 feet and about to plunge into the Irish Sea. They were very touching. But Richard had the ability to compartmentalise issues in his brain. He could mentally bury previous experiences and concentrate on new projects.

To announce the first hot air balloon flight over the Valley of the Kings we went to Hyde Park and inflated a large royal blue balloon emblazoned, in gold, with the famous mask of Tutankhamun. I dressed Richard up in an Arab nobleman's attire and sat him on a camel. The press came out in force.

It took two years of solid work to produce all of the operating and maintenance manuals and enter them into Egyptian law. Once all of the licences, certifications, permits and myriad protocol driven approvals were in place, including those for the test flights in the Valley of the Kings, we turned to the pilot roster. We needed to appoint a chief pilot.

Luxor could be considered, by many, as a hardship post. I had negotiated a deal with the newly built Hilton hotel in Karnak, so the chief pilot's accommodation and food would be up to western standard, but other operating conditions would be tough. The pilot had to liaise with the booking agent and, weather permitting, fly passengers both in the mornings, entailing a 5am start, and in the afternoons. He had to train the constantly changing ground crew, supervise fuelling of the butane/nitrogen gas mix, maintain the balloon and carry out running repairs. It was a long day, seven days a week, the only breaks being when it was too windy to fly.

All of our company pilots were extremely busy flying the 50 odd balloons in our stable and would only be used in Luxor as relief pilots.

An Australian bush pilot, Graham, applied for the job and we flew him to the UK for the interview. He was used to flying in Australia in hot dusty conditions and seemed an ideal candidate. He was also very presentable and seemed to have a suitable personality and the necessary patience to deal with tourists and the frustrations of the Egyptian bureaucracy. I took him on a flight over Shropshire to make sure he had the requisite flying skills. He was a very accomplished pilot.

His licence, experience and medical certificates were all correct and I had no hesitation in appointing him. The system we had put in place in Egypt was simple. The Egyptian Aviation Authority would accept the British CAA (Civil Aviation Authority) licence and would issue an Egyptian licence on the back of that - once the pilots had undertaken a medical examination. The Aussie was a commercially rated pilot, having passed the stringent medical examinations associated with that, so it was not a problem. It just needed a rubber stamp.

We dispatched Graham to Egypt with all of the kit. He would fly to Cairo to complete the formalities of obtaining his Egyptian licence and medical certificate, and then on to Luxor to begin the unforgettable experience of fulfilling people's dreams of flying in a balloon over the most stunning desert and Nile landscapes and some of the most important historical monuments in the world.

Two days later I was urgently called by Muhammad, our operations manager in Luxor. He was talking very quickly in a highly agitated manner, what I would describe as full panic mode. 'Mr Mike, Mr Mike, the pilot you sent. He is no good. We have problem.'

I was not that alarmed. Problems in Egypt are par for the course and could be fixed. In fact many problems did not exist at all but they liked to find 'problems' and then 'fix' them to demonstrate how good they were. I called it the Egyptian merry-go-round; they just sat you on it, going around in ever decreasing circles until they found a solution.

So I said 'Muhammad, calm down. I'm sure you can solve the problem.'

'No Mr Mike, I cannot. Very sorry. He cannot fly in Egypt. Ever. Very sorry to say this to you Mr Mike.'

'OK, what is the problem?' I asked.

'He failed his medical, here in Cairo,' said Muhammad.

I explained that this was not possible. That he was a fully qualified commercial pilot with all the medical certificates, now recognised by the Egyptian authorities.

'No Mr Mike.' Muhammad urgently explained. 'He failed the medical because of his left leg.'

'What the hell's wrong with his left leg?' I asked.

'He hasn't got one!' cried Muhammad.

'What?'

'Well he does have one,' said Muhammad, 'but it's a wood one. He took it off and put it on the doctor's desk. The doctor was very angry Mr Mike. It is not my fault Mr Mike. Why you send us a pilot without a leg? The doctor asked him to walk in a straight line but he can only hop! Please speak to Captain Graham, I give him the phone.'

I slowly realised what had happened and I was beside myself with anger when Graham came to the telephone. 'G'day Mike, this is a bit of a fubar isn't it?' (for the uninitiated FUBAR is a term used when things are Fucked Up Beyond All Recognition). I thought I could sense a smile, the way you can sometimes when someone is talking on the telephone.

'Graham,' I asked, 'are you an amputee?'

'Yeah mate,' he said. 'Lost it in a car accident when I was eight. Never been an issue before mate.'

'Well it's an effing issue now, mate! Why didn't you tell me?'

'You never asked, mate.'

And he was right, I didn't ask. It did not occur to me. I can imagine the conversation. 'Well, Graham, you fly well, have all the experience we need, all the correct licences and medical certificates. By the way, how many legs have you got?' I knew I was facing a battle I could not win. It would be impossible to get the Egyptian's to change their rules. It could take years. I told him to get the first flight out.

BV - #0035 - 171019 - C0 - 234/156/11 - PB - 9781780913834